Praise for

WHY NOT TODAY

Why Not Today is a vitally important book for our generation. If we do not take this global scourge seriously, we will be as though we did nothing about slavery, segregation, apartheid or other historical injustices. This book will open minds and hearts to one of the most important issue of our day. Please take time to read it. Then get copies to give to your friends.

DR. GEORGE VERWER | *Author, World Missions Advocate*

I know Friends Church and have spoken there. It's a dynamic congregation that doesn't just preach the Gospel, but lives the Gospel. I love what it's doing to help release a generation of boys and girls still known as "the lowest of the low." This is Christ helping us live out justice and mercy, speaking out for people with no voice. Whether India grabs you by the sleeve or Christ does—or both!—here is a great book about one man whose response was: Why not today?

GOVERNOR MIKE HUCKABEE

I resonate with Matthew Cork's story, well told in the pages of *Why Not Today*. It reads like a novel, taking us into his world as a leader and into the movement that is changing India. This vision of freedom transformed Matthew's role as a leader. It transformed a growing army of people just like you who are standing up for the cause of the Dalits. Matthew introduces our mutual friend Dr. Joseph D'souza, who now plays a prophetic role in the transformation of a nation. You will be inspired, taught, encouraged and most of all, prompted to get involved.

ANDREW SCOTT | *President, Operation Mobilization USA*

My friend and alumnus of Azusa Pacific University, Matthew Cork, has written a compelling story about leadership and the power of vision. More importantly, this story shines a bright light on the dark side of the burgeoning global economy: the widespread violation of human rights. Our students serve worldwide, and I am proud to say that this new emerging generation is uniquely prepared to become a voice for the voiceless. This book will inspire and energize this new generation to change the world for good.

JON R. WALLACE | *President, Azusa Pacific University*

It was the great missionary to India, William Carey, who said, "Expect great things from God; attempt great things for God." This book, *Why Not Today*, does both. I read it just as I anticipated my first trip to India and, because of this book from Matthew and Ken, I know I will go with a heart more in tune with God's heart for the plight of the Dalits.

WAYNE SHEPHERD | *Radio Host*

Matthew Cork captures you with his honest vulnerability. Matthew allowed himself to be wrecked by the disparity of what he saw and experienced in India. An emotionally driven, bold declaration was backed up by integrity and perseverance through a journey of twists and turns as he and his team sought to make a difference in the plight of the Dalits. As a result, multitudes will be challenged to see people with different eyes and take action.

MARY FRANCES BOWLEY | *CEO/President of Wellspring Living, author of* The White Umbrella

Why read *Why Not Today?* Because a pastor went from being a Christian to a Christ-follower, and the difference is big. For starters, you open to real risk—to geography that outstrips your comfort zone. You're not just about the church anymore, you're about the world. You're getting over what Matthew Cork calls the "virus of religiosity" to be part of what Jesus is doing all over the globe. And there's no better place to be.

BOB ROBERTS | *Founder and Senior Pastor, Northwood Church, author of* Bold as Love

Why Not Today powerfully describes the impact that one church in this country can have when they wholeheartedly commit to make a difference. You will be challenged to take a personal inventory on what you can do to end this stain on all of humanity.

CATHEY ANDERSON | *Founder, Freedom Climb*

Don't read this book unless you are prepared to be disturbed, inspired, and awakened to a new world inside and outside of yourself. It happened to my friend Matthew Cork; and I'll warn you in advance, his passion is contagious. His story will not leave you in a dark place, but will lift you to a place that is strategic, exciting, and purposeful.

GENE APPEL | *Senior Pastor, Eastside Christian Church, Anaheim, CA*

WHY NOT TODAY

TRAFFICKING, SLAVERY,
THE GLOBAL CHURCH...
AND YOU

MATTHEW CORK
and **KENNETH KEMP**

MOODY PUBLISHERS

CHICAGO

All Scripture quotations, unless otherwise indicated, are taken from the Holy Bible, New International Version®, NIV®. Copyright ©1973, 1978, 1984 by Biblica, Inc.™ Used by permission of Zondervan. All rights reserved worldwide.

Scripture quotations marked NKJV are taken from the *New King James Version*. Copyright © 1982 by Thomas Nelson, Inc. Used by permission. All rights reserved.

Scripture quotations marked NLT are taken from the *Holy Bible, New Living Translation*, copyright © 1996, 2004. Used by permission of Tyndale House Publishers, Inc., Wheaton, Illinois 60189, USA. All rights reserved.

Published in association with the literary agency of Wolgemuth & Associates, Inc.

Edited by Elizabeth Cody Newenhuyse
Cover design: Erik M. Peterson
Cover images: Girl and slum image © Kenneth Kemp
Interior design: Smartt Guys design
Photo for Matthew Cork: Frenzel Studios

Library of Congress Cataloging-in-Publication Data

Cork, Matthew.
Why not today : trafficking, slavery, the global church and you / Matthew Cork, Kenneth Kemp ; [foreword by] Joseph D'souza.
     pages cm
Summary: "Three hundred million - that's the number of people subjected to slavery, sex-trafficking, discrimination, and unspeakable poverty in India. That's the same number of people as live in the entire United States. They are the Dalit people, the untouchables. When Matthew Cork, a California pastor, first encountered the Dalits he was shaken to his core. He learned that Gandhi's success at bringing about freedom did not extend to freeing the Dalits from the bondage of the Caste system that has oppressed them for centuries. Cork was moved to commit his church to partner with The Dalit Freedom Network to build 200 schools over ten years, a commitment of over 20 million dollars. And they are doing it. The movement has gained such momentum that a dramatic, feature-length film, Not Today (Nottodaythemovie.com) is being produced and promoted by the same group that did so for Courageous, Facing the Giants, and Fireproof. This book tells story of the Dalit people and the rising efforts to set them free, in both soul and society. It is a story of both brokenness and hope, of oppression and freedom. It calls the reader to join in the movement to freedom and restoration. The Dalits need your help. Why not start today?"-- Provided by publisher.
Includes bibliographical references.
ISBN 978-0-8024-1083-2 (pbk.)
1. Dalits--India--Social conditions. 2. Dalits--Abuse of--India. 3. Caste-based discrimination--India. I. Kemp, Kenneth, 1948- II. Title.
HT720.C67 2013
305.5'6880954--dc23
                              2013012686

All websites and phone numbers listed herein are accurate at the time of publication but may change in the future or cease to exist. The listing of website references and resources does not imply publisher endorsement of the site's entire contents. Groups and organizations are listed for informational purposes, and listing does not imply publisher endorsement of their activities.

We hope you enjoy this book from Moody Publishers. Our goal is to provide high-quality, thought-provoking books and products that connect truth to your real needs and challenges. For more information on other books and products written and produced from a biblical perspective, go to www.moodypublishers.com or write to:

Moody Publishers
820 N. La Salle Boulevard
Chicago, IL 60610

1 3 5 7 9 10 8 6 4 2

Printed in the United States of America

Dedicated to

The Generous, Devoted People of
Friends Church

The Dalit People
Especially the Children
Free Indeed

Contents

Foreword

TODAY WE ARE WITNESSING a pivotal moment in history.

For three thousand years, one dominant religion branded more than one-fourth of our nation's population as subhuman. Estimates vary, but those who study the facts number this group, known as "Dalits" or "untouchables," to be somewhere between 200 and 300 million. Historically, any interaction between this alienated group and the mainstream has been met with harsh penalties, even violence. Separatism has been the accepted norm. It puts our nation in a league with South Africa's old apartheid and some of the worst systems of slavery in the world.

Even the most skilled wordsmiths have difficulty describing the heavy impact of this monstrous oppression. It weighs heavily on the mind, heart, and soul of the victims of caste. Belief in reincarnation provides little hope. Hunger, disease, ignorance, self-hatred, cruel discrimination, backbreaking labor, sexual abuse, human trafficking, injury, and social withdrawal are lifelong companions to those who are called "outcaste"— or "untouchable."

When my country won its independence from the British in 1948, a new constitution declared religious freedom. More than sixty years later, the hope of freedom remains largely out of reach for Dalits. India is emerging as a leading contributor to the global economic community, but too many of our people are left behind.

But things are changing.

In 2001, our team made a deliberate decision to join a wide coalition of activists who proclaim and promote the right of religious choice for all, including Dalits. It was a powerful breakthrough on many levels.

We firmly believe that the liberation of the Dalit population as free and equal will require nothing short of a miracle. To be sustainable, we also understand that young Dalits must have access to high-quality education. They need English, the language of commerce. But they have been denied access to any form of upward mobility. As we proclaim religious freedom, we also share the kingdom message of Jesus Christ. People have the right, the ability, and the responsibility to make their choice. There is no coercion. But as millions have come alive to a freedom long withheld, tens of thousands have chosen to follow Jesus. My good friend Matthew Cork appeared in my office for our first meeting just as the momentum began to accelerate.

I'm very pleased to say, the movement is now expanding beyond our wildest dreams. Churches and schools are springing up all over India. We consider the words of Jesus to be central to the message: "If the Son will set you free, you will be free indeed." A whole new generation is embracing this freedom in unprecedented numbers.

When folks come from all over the world to visit us—to see our schools, visit the slums, get acquainted with our people—God seems to impact them deeply. Matthew Cork was no exception. I could tell from the start that this man of vision saw things that many miss. When he came for the first time, his people in Yorba Linda, California, had already made a substantial commitment to our cause. As you will read, Matthew's heart was prepared. Thanks to his eyes to see, his heart to feel, and his spirit that radiates enthusiasm, that commitment multiplied. In this partnership with his friend and cowriter Ken Kemp, they have captured the story of the movement.

It is one thing to be moved to action. It is quite another to keep the momentum alive and with sustained commitment take an entire movement to new levels. In the years we have worked together, Matthew and his people have delivered what they promised. Their partnership has been invaluable. They have become true world-changers.

Great movements of God are often born out of pain, disappointment, and broken dreams. Matthew Cork's story is the candid portrayal of a church and a ministry that nearly imploded. Maybe this is why Matthew and I understand each other so well. We both have been on our knees, perplexed, pleading that God would move hearts.

We are living examples. Those prayers have been answered, yet there remains much to do. We are still on our knees. Now, not alone, but together. This is only the beginning.

Everyone who cares about freedom, justice, redemption, reconciliation, and vision will find in these pages encouragement, motivation, and direction. The cause of Dalit Freedom inspires true liberation all over the world. You will be energized as you engage the background of our movement and the rebirth of a church that nearly lost its way. But most important, you will see how one person can change the world. The next person to do so may be you.

When you finish reading, pass along this book to a friend. Together, we can accomplish the impossible.

DR. JOSEPH D'SOUZA
President, Dalit Freedom Network
President, All India Christian Council

Introduction

I LIVE IN A COUNTRY where most citizens, according to pollsters, claim to be Christian. A full 78 percent of the population makes that claim. [1]

I am not sure what that means to all those people. I can only speak from personal experience.

For many years, like most Americans, I claimed to be a Christian, too. I grew up in a Christian home, went to church every time the doors were open, played Christian music, went to a Christian college, married a Christian girl. I work in a Christian church.

All that would make me a poster child for "Christian." Guys like me inflate the statistics.

It took something radical to shake me up. I bore the name. I had grown comfortable with the label. But I was not a follower of Jesus Christ.

I was unaware of the contradiction. What I really needed was something that went well beyond the routines that kept me in my little zone of comfort. I needed to be healed from the virus of religiosity. Rather than conforming to the expectations that surrounded me (many a product of my own imagination), I needed to be transformed: from the predictable regimens of religion to becoming an authentic follower of Christ. It took awhile. But I learned that simply identifying myself as a Christian was a lot more comfortable than becoming a disciple. That is what needed changing.

For thirty-eight years, this was the life I knew. Then Jesus showed up.

This is why I wrote this book. When I asked my friend Ken Kemp to work with me to produce these pages, he jumped right in. We have worked closely together over these past several years. Ken is a history buff. As we collaborated on the book, he helped me pull together much of the background of the movement so essential to our story. As we share our personal story, we also fill in the detail that has made Dalit freedom a global cause. In the process of writing this firsthand account, we have relived the most significant days of my life. It has all happened in the context of an historic movement—we believe, a movement of God.

> I had no idea that when I went to the other side of the world, I would find what I was missing.

But it is not really about me. What happened to me can happen to anyone. It can happen to you. If it has not already, I want you to learn what I have learned. It has made all the difference. I had no idea that when I went to the other side of the world, I would find what I was missing.

Like me, you may have grown up surrounded by good Christian influence. But it is also possible that you had none of the benefits of a wholesome, healthy upbringing. When you read about "untouchables," you may well relate. All your life, you have felt like an untouchable; as though you are at odds with the rest of the world. You know loneliness. Emptiness. Rejection. Hopelessness.

Either way, poster-child Christian or seeker, there is something here for you. How do I know? Read what follows. Judge for yourself.

About the time I considered myself to have it all figured out, tragedy struck. My mother-in-law, Mardi's mom, passed away. Then my father-in-law, her dad, died shortly after. Then I lost my job. Our third child, a daughter, Ella, was born. It was the most intense year of our lives. Mardi looked at me and said, "We'll be OK." She seemed convinced. But I was not so sure.

I had planned adequately, or so I thought. I was a comfortable Christian, serving in an affluent church. But the comfort blinded me to so much. Then, it all seemed to collapse. Beyond my control. Without warning. In my pain, God brought clarity. "Get up," Jesus told a broken man, "take up your bed and walk!" I learned that message was for me, too.

The proverbs made more sense to me than ever before. "I guide you in the way of wisdom and lead you along straight paths. When you walk, your steps will not be hampered; when you run, you will not stumble."[2] Once again, it was as though Solomon's words were written just for me.

When the Bible says, "Speak up for those who cannot speak for themselves; ensure justice for those being crushed. Yes, speak up for the poor and helpless, and see that they get justice."[3] I began to realize that I had missed something. I had not considered it indifference or neglect, but it was both. It was time for me to look beyond the comfort, beyond the excess, beyond the self-absorption, and take a hard look at a world in need.

I had convinced myself that someone else would do that. It wasn't my concern. I have a church to run, budgets to manage, staff to lead—basically I have more important things to do. But I had to face the facts. If I would follow Jesus, I would have to change. That would be painful.

Bill Hybels once asked a profound question: "Do you have a vision worth dying for?"

A vision? I barely had a church, let alone a vision. But I started to pray. I asked God to give me something worth dying for. Another building program was not it.

About one year after I came back to the church, I approved the request to build two schools in India. They would provide Dalit children, the outcasts of the Hindu caste system, an education. Our missions pastor brought an ambitious proposal. "Let's build ten schools in five years," he said with conviction. I wanted to be a visionary, so I said, "No, let's make that twenty."

Looking back, I had no idea whatsoever what I was saying back then. Jay Hoff and I laugh now, when we remember that conversation. Since that crazy day, my world has been rocked. Everything has changed.

Best of all, I now have a vision worth dying for.

My favorite verse comes from Paul's letter to the church in Ephesus. I am crazy enough to believe it. "Now to Him who is able to do exceedingly abundantly above all that we ask or think, according to the power that works in us, to Him be glory in the church by Christ Jesus to all generations."[4]

If you are already a follower of Jesus, then you will understand. If you are not, that's all right. If you are turned off by religion, believe me, I understand. Read what follows. It will help you see there is a major difference between religion and relationship.

When I read those words in Paul's letter, I had a new set of eyes to see and new ears to hear. When you become a follower of Jesus and His teachings, when you have enough courage to lay aside your mat, whatever it is, sickness, unbelief, doubt, fear, indifference, or just plain laziness, your life will be forever changed. Jesus says, lay it down. Trust Me. I will blow you away. I will do more than you could ever imagine. "Get up, take your mat and walk."[5]

That was for me.

I want to take you on this journey with me. When I set out to do the things I believed were my responsibilities as a Christian, I did not comprehend the scope of God's plan for the world. I did not understand that religion gets mixed in, and sometimes blurs God's kingdom perspective. I'm still learning. In these pages, I will share my experience with the church and how we came near collapse and calamity. My role as a pastor transitioned from a job to a calling. For a difficult period, I believed I had lost everything I worked so hard to gain. But then, in a hotel room in

India, I realized I was hanging on to the wrong stuff. I found something better; much, much better.

About the Dalit Freedom story, I had a lot to learn. You do, too. We will take you to India and introduce you to some of the heroes who have committed their lives to freedom's cause. Some have made the ultimate sacrifice for the Gospel. There has been documented, terrifying persecution. There is resistance to change. I want to walk with you and share with you a firsthand account of the courageous, visionary, and determined leadership that Dr. Joseph D'souza and his team have exhibited and still bring. God is raising up an army of workers. It's happening. The nation is changing.

One of the biggest surprises for me on this journey was the radical suggestion that we produce a full-length feature film. *Not Today* has been seen in theaters across the country. The DVD will have a global reach. I want you to know the story of how the film came about; how it was made; the people who contributed time, money, and talent to make it a powerful motivational tool to mobilize an even greater army. It may inspire you to do something outrageously effective, contributing to the expansion of God's work in the world. As we take this journey together, you will meet the writers, the producer and director, our actors and volunteers as we take you behind the scenes. Our main characters are Caden and Annika. We are Caden—indifferent and self-absorbed. We meet Annika—a lost little girl caught in a web of cruelty. In what becomes an obsession to find and rescue (redeem) Annika, Caden finds himself, just like we found *ourselves*.

And after all, isn't that what Jesus talked about?

The best is yet to come. Here is my prayer for you. It is a Franciscan benediction quoted by Philip Yancey:[6]

May God bless you with discomfort at easy answers, half-truths, and superficial relationships, so that you may live deep within your heart.

May God bless you with anger at injustice, oppression, and exploitation; so that you may work for justice, freedom and peace.

May God bless you with tears to shed for those who suffer from pain, rejection, starvation and war; so that you may reach out to comfort them and to turn their pain into joy.

And may God bless you with enough foolishness to believe that you can make a difference in this world, so that you can do what others will surely say cannot be done.

Amen.

So here is my encouragement to you: *Get up, take your mat and walk.*

MATTHEW CORK

January 2013

NOTES

1. In 1948, 91 percent of Americans identified with a Christian faith. Twenty years ago, in 1989, 82 percent of Americans identified as Christian; in 1999, it was 84 percent. A 2009 Gallup Poll found that 78 percent of all American adults identified with Christian faith.
2. Proverbs 4:11–12.
3. Proverbs 31:8–9 (NLT).
4. Ephesians 3:20–21 (NKJV).
5. Mark 2:9.
6. Philip Yancey, *Prayer: Does It Make Any Difference?* (Grand Rapids: Zondervan, 2006), 105.

Chapter 1

VISION

BEGUMPET INTERNATIONAL AIRPORT is no longer operational. For many years it served the seven million people of Hyderabad, the City of Pearls, from the center of the metropolis in the heart of India. Begumpet's runway was large enough to accommodate Air Force One when President George W. Bush visited the city in 2006. But they shut it down. Today a new modern airport buzzes around the clock in Hyderabad. A new India is emerging.

Several years ago, when I arrived at that old airport, I believed our team was on to something important. We were on a mission. I pulled together a band of eight knowledgeable, smart, good people. And here we were, halfway around the world, on final approach in the middle of the night to touch down at Begumpet International Airport in a city once known as Bhagyanagaram, in the state of Andhra Pradesh. Before this trip, I had not even heard of Hyderabad.

I have traveled. I have seen hardship. But nothing prepared me for what I was about to see and hear and feel as the wheels thumped against the concrete and squealed on impact while the big jet engines roared, reversing their thrust and braking us to a stop on the runway of Begumpet International in Hyderabad, "The City of Pearls," Andhra Pradesh, India.

Prayer is part of my life. It is not a ritual. Not a routine. It is a lifeline. As the flight attendant in a distinctly Indian version of English told us all to remain seated, I have a talk with God, right there from my cramped passenger seat. I tell Him that I am open. I want Him to show me something of Himself. I ask Him to make me aware of the needs and hopes and aspirations of the people I will meet; that I will somehow see them as He does. That I will learn something. Something powerful.

I look over at my friend and colleague Jay Hoff. We grin and nod. "We're here" is the unspoken message. "Can you believe it?"

FROM CALIFORNIA TO ANDHRA PRADESH

As the doors open and the pressurized cabin draws in the air from outside at ground level, I get my first sensory experience of India. There's a heaviness about that Indian air; humidity blending with the smoke of burning embers, the hint of rich spices, and the scent of human bodies that live without much fresh water, moving day after day up and down the crowded streets of the sweltering city.

Little boys and girls, some of them barely eight years old, emerge from the shadows selling trinkets and candies and chewing gum.

I'm a Californian, used to sunshine and breezes. The Los Angeles smog is diminished, they tell me, thanks to several decades of stringent pollution-control measures. So when I draw in that first lungful of India air, I know I have entered a new world—of smells, of pollution, of overcrowding. It signals a change in paradigm. Time for me to let go of everything I have brought with me; to shed prejudices and biases and this American superiority complex inbred by too much American-made television. Time has come for me to let it go as I walk onto the tarmac in the dark of night and transition physically, mentally, and spiritually from California to Andhra Pradesh.

When I enter into the dilapidated terminal, even after midnight, the lobby clamors with commerce. The rental car counters, the shops, the newsstands, all crowded into every nook and cranny of space. Before long, a gang of young children approach. Clunker television sets flicker, pulling in their weak signal with rabbit-ear antennas. Little boys and girls, some of them barely eight or nine years old, emerge noisily from the shadows selling trinkets and candies and chewing gum. If they are not selling, they are begging.

"Money money! Help me! *Pleeeeeze!* One dolla! Uncle! PLEEEEZE!"

Another holds up a green pack of Wrigley's spearmint. "Gum? One dolla!" Then he pulls out a chocolate bar. "Candy? One dolla."

It is clearly a familiar routine. All of them are skilled, eager, charming. They tap their lips with their fingertips signaling hunger. Then they touch their bellies. They repeat the motion.

"Money money! *Pleeeeeze!* Help me! One dolla. PLEEEEZE! Uncle. Uncle!"

"No," I snap. "Not today." I was not very convincing.

One of our hosts sees my dilemma. He steps up.

The airport lobby is filled with upscale business travelers, most of them Indian. They wear blue and gray and black suits and carry expensive leather briefcases, stacked atop a carry-on bag on rollers pulled by an extended handle. One slaps shut his cellphone and slips it into his vest pocket. He turns, looks at me and then at the children. He looks away in disgust. He seems to be embarrassed that a visitor to his country would be accosted this way.

Then our personal host moves into protective mode. "Go away!" he says firmly, and he waves his hand signaling that there will be no money. The children step back. But only momentarily. They turn briefly to the businessman. He is outnumbered. They gesture him with a snarl. He growls.

The chorus of youngsters turns back to our host. "Go away!" he declares. "No money." He repeats it three or four times.

The leader of the pack delivers some impertinent message to our host I cannot decipher. I am certain it is insulting. They turn to the man in the suit. They repeat the gesture. He throws his hands into the air and continues on his way, head wagging.

The children go back to their mission, chasing after someone else in the crowd. "Money money! Help me! Pleeeeeze!" tapping their mouths and stomachs.

Our orientation session had prepared us for this assault. I turn to our host.

"Dalits?" I ask with slight hesitation.

"Dalits," he replies.

We were told beforehand to ignore the children. It was a simple survival technique. I did my background reading. I knew about child trafficking and the heartbreaking fact that these children were not simply street-smart entrepreneurs. They are the sole property of child abusers who release the kids on the streets where they meet up with foreigners who have money in their pockets.

> Who holds them when they cry? What kinds of cruelty are they exposed to? The questions close in on me as I try to ignore their calls for help.

Whatever they might extract from pedestrians on their way to do business goes directly into the coffers of the ringleader. The lost children are thus cash machines for their "guardians."

For my own sanity's sake, I force myself to avoid eye contact. I just keep walking ahead. I am a father myself. By personal experience, I am a firsthand witness to the miracle of childbirth. The woman I love and respect delivered those three children of ours. I watched it happen, and in that moment of awe, something clicked. The overwhelming wonder of it all awakened me to the sanctity of life and as a father, instilled in me the instinct to protect even if it cost me my own life. The prospect that any harm might come to any one of our children causes me to jump involuntarily into action. I see all children differently now that I have my own.

So, surrounded by these little people, grabbing at my arm, pleading, I wonder. Where do they sleep? What do they eat? What are they learning? Who patches up their skinned knees and elbows? Who holds them when they cry? What kinds of cruelty are they exposed to? These questions close in on me as I try to ignore their calls for help, and keep from meeting their wide, eager eyes with mine. All at once I see their captivating smiles . . . their laughter, tinged with a streak of street-mean . . . their childish warmth and big-city hardness, all at once. And so many of them fiercely competing for my "dolla."

I keep on walking. A sadness settles in. I see my team moving alongside me, their luggage in tow. I know they are thinking the very same thing. But we don't speak about it until later.

After the chaos of the airport and the city streets, traffic jams even in the dead of night, the hotel is a welcome sight. But after my encounter with the street kids and the sights of the crowded city, I feel uneasy with the opulence at the entrance. Marble floors and walls. Extravagant chandeliers. Fresh-cut flowers bursting out of colorful vases on glass-topped tables; leather seating in conversational groupings in a large space with a high ceiling. Well-dressed staff welcome me with a warm smile, offering assistance and directing me to my comfortable room. After a twenty-hour flight and a journey across multiple time zones, it all comes together in a perfect storm of sensory impact. I jump into the shower and then drop into bed between clean, crisp sheets. The pillow is soft. My whole body, relaxed. And then I hear it. Those little voices. "Money money! *One dolla! . . . Help me! . . . Pleeeeze!* Just one dolla."

They tap their lips, then their stomachs. Their eyes plead.

I fall asleep.

THE MAN WITH THE BROKEN HEART

The next day, we make our way to the mission headquarters. Along the way, I see scores of aging women hunched over brooms, sweeping sidewalks and gutters and entryways. The deep lines on their expressionless faces betray the years of empty, menial labor. I point to a group of them and ask our driver, "Dalits?"

He nods. "Dalits."

I can't take my eyes away from them. Meanwhile, the words of the children continue to echo in my head.

During our ride to the mission, city gives way to the countryside, but the poverty doesn't end. We eventually reach our destination and amid the silence in our group's vehicle, I know for sure the fact that every mind is racing, every heart is being torn in two.

Getting out of the car and climbing the stairs, we begin our "official" visit. There is a man waiting for us who will turn my life inside out.

Dr. Joseph D'souza is an imposing presence. Under a shock of jet-black hair, carefully cut and combed, impeccably groomed, he strikes an air of confidence and purpose. His handshake is warm as he locks eyes with mine.

"So you are Pastor Matthew Cork," he says in a strong, cheerful voice. I introduce my team. He knows several of them from previous visits.

Seated in a simple but nicely appointed conference room, there are some twenty-five of us around the table, eight from our California group. Dr. D'souza focuses on the task at hand. I pull my notebook and pen out of my travel case. I know I am in the presence of an extraordinary man. Several years before, our church had committed to supporting his work. I was here to learn and observe more.

For thirty-five years, he served the people of India as a Christian missionary. Just a few years ago, he went through a transformation that had profound implications.

Dr. D'souza's Christianity was considered by most to be a Western intrusion, a distinctly foreign brand of religion held in disdain by the universities, ignored by politicians, and viewed as a threat by established Indian religious leaders. The work to which he had dedicated his life had made only painfully slow progress. From my preparation for this meeting, I understood that his heart had broken as he contemplated the plight of the "untouchables," the millions of Indians branded as "Dalits," robbed of human dignity and condemned to a lifetime of abject poverty with no hope of ever breaking out of this cruel bondage. The longer he lived among these people, the more he understood the nature of an endemic and ancient injustice and the deeper his commitment grew to becoming an agent of change.

In that conference room on the first day of our visit, I learned that part of his radical transformation and commitment to the Dalit people came even in his family life. He married a Dalit: Mariam. Later, I heard the full story. Her beauty. Her smile. Her quick wit. Her elegant features. The sound of her voice energized him in ways he'd never known. Society stood against them, though. The prohibitions against such a marriage, drilled into his mind and heart from childhood . . . well, they were powerful.

> He contemplated the plight of the "untouchables," the millions of Indians robbed of human dignity and condemned to a lifetime of abject poverty.

However, the moment he realized he was in love with her, for the first time in his life, he simultaneously felt a smoldering, nearly uncontainable rage over caste-based and racial injustice. He couldn't look back; his commitment to this woman and to her people was forever secured. He rebelled against the traditional cultural mandates and, as a result, paid a heavy personal price. His parents. The extended family. Some of his friends. His siblings. His professors. They all shook their heads in disapproval. "Shame," they said.

He didn't care. What a prize. He never looked back. On their wedding day, a family was born—and also, a destiny.

That day, we get around to the specifics of this destiny—for the D'souzas, and, I would come to find out, for me. In 2001, Joseph recalls, everything changed, transforming his work from a quiet and steady operation of a few hundred dedicated Indian Christians into a national movement with a high profile encompassing the lives of thousands and thrusting him onto the global scene. A few years later we had joined with financial support. But we did not know all his vision, nor all of Andhra Pradesh's (and indeed India's) need for change.

Dr. D'souza makes a major statement of fact that takes me by surprise: "The work we are contemplating has historic social consequence. The initiatives will have national implications for millions of people in the emerging generation. A coalition of leaders from many religious and political backgrounds have come together to urge the eradication of a system that has crushed the spirit of an entire people for hundreds, maybe thousands of years. This is a critical moment in the history of all of India."

Then he turns to me in a serious and deliberate tone. "Pastor Cork, your church is the largest congregation that has come to support us. You are from the most capable nation on the face of the earth. A full 20 percent of our available resources for our work among the Dalit people come from your people in California. You have stood alongside to help us change the course of history. We could not do this without you. We are deeply grateful. Thank you."

> Dalits are not considered human. They are used and abused, and they have no recourse or avenues toward justice.

His piercing look rivets me to my seat. The passion in his eyes is compelling. Palpable. The others in the room feel it, too. Silence.

To help us more greatly understand the movement and all its components, he gives us a primer on the Hindu caste system. When Mahatma Gandhi galvanized the nation over sixty years ago and won national independence from the British, the caste system's practice of "untouchability" was declared illegal. But the new laws were inadequate and never enforced. The permanent branding of the Dalits and other "low-caste" people remained firmly in place. Separate drinking fountains. Separate bathroom facilities. Denied access to restaurants and hotels.

Dalits are expected to perform the most base of all social functions: caring for human waste, animal waste, discarded trash. Dalits are not considered human. They get no education. They are used and abused in the shadowy back alleys of the cities and the deep recessed forests of the rural villages, and have no recourse or avenues toward justice. There is no protection from law enforcement, no access to the courts, no political voice, no hope of upward mobility.

I sit speechless. I learn that the caste system and its practices are monstrously multifaceted—socially, politically, spiritually. Dr. D'souza goes on to relate how Christians in India have refused to stand idly by and have joined forces with others from differing backgrounds to address the injustice. Together they demand that everyone in all parts of society, from government officials to business professionals to academic leaders, join hands to eradicate discrimination in all its destructive forms. India must recognize this enormous human resource—the Dalit people—and open wide the doors of opportunity. "I have committed my life to this cause," he declares.

As D'souza continues, however, his tone shifts from staunch determination to resolute sadness. "We've lost this generation." There is an audible sigh as he looks to the floor. He pauses, then looks up. "But there is hope for the next generation."

I understand what he means. For Dalits over the age of twenty, the system has created devastating consequences: Dignity? Violated. Caste-based identity? Locked in. Basic education? Beyond reach. Subsistence trumps freedom. Tragically, adults in the Dalit community are conditioned to accept these atrocities as normal.

But a new generation is coming. It is the children, D'souza says, the children—*they* are the future. These young minds can absorb new possibilities.

They are hungry for knowledge. They respond to the message that they are fearfully and wonderfully made and that there is limitless potential beyond the squalid conditions of the neighborhood. As D'souza revs up the argument, I can hear the hope in his voice. He has seen this transformation firsthand. It is this remarkable transformation of individual lives that drives his aspirations for the future.

AN AUDACIOUS GOAL

"We have an audacious goal. I never imagined I would think in these terms." He pauses for a moment. "Over the next ten years, we intend to build *one thousand schools* for Dalit children." His emphasis is unmistakable.

He continues, filling in the detail. Then he makes his case. Clearly the vision possesses him and goes beyond logical human reasoning. Yet it has the power to lift up an entire population.

Upon hearing the enormous magnitude of this vision, this cause, this calling, a stark realization finally hits me. Did Dr. D'souza really say that our church's involvement represents a full 20 *percent* of all that was already happening with the Dalits? I was astounded that our church could make such a significant difference. We were changing lives; freeing the next generation. And at that point, we really hadn't sacrificed much at all. I had not yet challenged our people, compelled them to give. We had not yet communicated that we had a vision worth dying for. At that point, *I* did not have a vision worth dying for.

But that all is changing in this one moment as I and others from our group sit there with Dr. D'souza in an unprepossessing conference room in Hyderabad, India.

I sit silently, listening and seriously reflecting on the power of these thoughts. One thousand schools in ten years—that *can be* done. We *can* be a part. We *can* do 20 percent.

And then I do the unthinkable. I speak. All eyes are on me; Indians looking in my direction with anticipation and with gratitude for what we had already done. I could see it on their faces. And then it happens.

In a small voice, but with a spirit of deep conviction, I say it out loud. "We can be 20 percent of this great vision. We can be responsible for two hundred schools over the next ten years. We *can* do that." I repeat it. The conviction takes hold of me. "And we *will* do that for your people."

Instantly, the magnitude of what I say publicly hits me privately. In that moment, I had just committed our church to roughly *twenty million dollars* over the next ten years. Doubt floods my mind. Worry grips me. If I could take it back, I would. But I know God is in this place, in this commitment. This is God's deal. My role is to listen and be faithful. So I take a deep breath and put on a smile. My team looks at me: *Are you crazy?* But at the same time, I know God is in this.

In those few moments, it becomes clear. I know my life, my ministry, my focus—all of it—is changing. But I still don't see how profound it really is.

This is the way it is with God. The picture may not be clear. The "how-to" seems incomplete, but the vision is compelling. It touches you deep within your heart and there is only one choice: the way of obedience. Am I willing to move forward, believing God and His Word about faith, or do I sit on the sideline until all the questions are answered, all the doubts are cleared up and all the risks eliminated?

> "We can do that." The conviction takes hold of me. "And we *will* do that for your people."

The answer is clear, and I know what I have to do: I have no choice but to lead and to trust God with the results. I will be obedient, and I believe He will be faithful.

It starts to settle in and becomes personal. I, Matthew Cork, a pastor and former trumpet player from Missouri, am going to lead our church to be a part of something more significant than any of us could ever have imagined. We now have joined forces to bring freedom to *an entire people group*. It is a freedom that can liberate souls from the bondage of sin and death. It replaces despair with hope and life. It is freedom from injustice, slavery, poverty, freedom from a caste system that considers millions of human beings made in God's image as worthless . . . untouchable.

> I have been in India less than twenty-four hours. God has already rocked my world.

We have an open door, a platform to proclaim freedom to the minds of those who have been taught to see themselves as less than animals. We will play a part in bringing the ultimate eternal freedom of knowing this one called Jesus in a genuine and personal way. And as we play our part in what the Spirit is doing, God's church in our little town in Southern California will never be the same. I have been in India less than twenty-four hours. God has already rocked my world.

To this day, I do not know exactly what it was that came over me. I want to believe that it was a prompting from God. But I have been around long enough to know that I need others to help me sort out the difference between a holy moment and some personal impulse that is rooted in my own humanness. On the way out the door of the office, I grab Dr. D'souza by the elbow. He turns to me.

"My friend." I halt for a moment. "I want you to understand. What I said in the conference room is for real." Another pause. "As of today, I am committed to find the resources we need to build two hundred schools."

Dr. D'souza stops cold. Our eyes lock. His to mine, mine to his. A warm smile slowly expands, lighting up his face. I repeat my commitment with as much sincerity as I can muster. I extend my hand as confirmation. He takes it with both of his, and we exchange a handshake that signals a turning point for us both. It isn't one of those cartoonish, exaggerated handshakes born out of illusory enthusiasms. It is a firm, deliberate coming together of two men with the same passion to make things right. My eyes fill up with tears. I see the same in my new Indian friend as he sees his many years of seemingly unfruitful sacrifice begin to be rewarded. The slow progress of all these years is finally proving worth it all.

Releasing Dr. D'souza's grip and left alone for a moment as my group and I transition to the next of the day's activities, I take a deep, cleansing breath. Despite the overwhelming confirmation from our Indian partners and from the Spirit of God speaking to me so clearly, my emotions and feelings of doubt rage within me, swelling again like one of those unanticipated tsunamis.

"Cork," I ask myself. "Cork. What just happened? No approval of the elders. No consulting the congregation. You just put it out there. Have you confused the voice of God with intestinal rumbling? Are you simply caught up in the emotion and fatigue? Does this make any sense at all?" And then I did some simple math. I make one more quick calculation of the price tag on my verbal contract. *Twenty million dollars.* I repeat the number. Wow.

But repeating the figure over to myself in my head, instead of fear, I sense a deep confidence. And as crazy as it sounds, I feel no regret. Yes, a perceptible shiver went up my spine, but it wasn't anxiety. I guess we would call it belief.

And as all of these thoughts race through my mind, Dr. D'souza says, with a gleam in his eye, "Next, I must take you to one of the first schools built by your church." And with that, we pile into our bus and back out into the streets.

THE BRIGHT FLOWERS OF UDDAMARRI SCHOOL

Jostling about in the stop-and-go traffic and engulfed in the cacophony of sounds flooding in through the open bus windows, I can't take my eyes off the scene passing my window. The crowds. The rustic building materials. The slums. The people who go about their business up and down the swarming streets. I see it all now through fresh eyes; through the lens of my new friend and partner, Dr. D'souza.

Our bus pulls up to the entrance of the first of many villages that I would see in India. The scene before us still is the most profound picture in my mind to this day: Uddamarri School.

The contrast of this rural village scene against the streets and slums of the city hits me like a lightning bolt. I see bright, rich colors of flowers in the tiny manicured garden. There are students standing outside waiting. The school principal formally greets us. The teachers stand watch, their students lined up in rows like a marching band, all dressed alike. Blue trousers for the boys, jumper skirts for the girls. Matching checkered shirts and blouses, held together by neckties and scarves. The children are groomed; clean hair and bright smiles.

A banner hangs on the wall. "WELCOME PASTOR MATTHEW CORK." At first, I am embarrassed. I am not the hero. That is for sure. My name is on the sign, but it is the folks back home who make this happen. It is also Dr. D'souza's diligence and indefatigable effort. And it is the teachers and the administrators and the community who came together to build this place against all odds. Yet here I am, greeted as a celebrity.

> The children begin to sing, and tears come to my eyes once again.

The principal steps forward and welcomes me with the same warmth and enthusiasm I felt from Dr. D'souza. He then offers a prayer: "Thank you for our friends in America. Thank you for their sacrifice. May we embrace the future that is now ours. And may we embrace them as they have embraced us."

The children begin to sing, and tears come to my eyes once again. I am moved by their voices: so joyful, you can feel the hope and anticipation. Sometimes I think I am cursed by this inescapable, easy emotion always on the surface. But in this case, no one mocks my expressive personality. They sing a familiar song of worship and gratitude. These are songs that I would sing as a child.

But one thing is clear: these children of Uddamarri School understand the meaning of these lyrics way more than I ever did. They sing out, "God is so good, God is so good, God is so good—He's so good to me." Tears roll down my cheeks. I do not feel worthy of this degree of affection.

It's at that emotionally charged moment that I flash back to Begumpet International Airport less than twenty-four hours before and that gaggle of street kids. "Help me! Money money! Uncle! One dolla! *Pleeeze!*" I recall their voices. And then my attention goes back to the students before me singing in full voice. *The contrast is stark. Street kids. Schoolkids.* What a difference. It steels my resolve.

The children beckon us to play in the yard. We kick a soccer ball. We high-five. Fist-pump. Our team shoots photos and then shows off the digital images. The children laugh.

Their English is not only understandable, it is lyrical and formal. "Hello sir, my name is … " I see respect. I feel honor. My natural instinct is to give both back.

"What would you like to be someday?" I ask. The answers coming from these Dalit children stun me. "I'm going to be a policeman." Another, "A teacher." Another, "A lawyer." "A doctor." "A pastor." I high-five each one for their ambitious plans.

We take a tour of the classrooms. The teachers have decorated the rooms as a serious learning environment. Science. Math. History. Reading. It is all there. On one wall, I see a motivational poster:

DO WHAT YOU CAN

WHERE YOU ARE

WITH WHAT YOU HAVE

It all comes together. Combine affection with nutrition with caring and competent teachers in an environment of support and encouragement. Then put all that on a strong spiritual foundation and children who would otherwise be cast aside or abused by a vicious system can become all they are meant to be.

THE CHILDREN OF PIPE VILLAGE

After our school visit, Dr. D'souza updates our plan. "After we freshen up, we must visit Pipe Village." I had heard of this place. I was eager to see the people inhabiting their unlikely residence. After a few hours, we arrive and I am greeted by the enthusiastic faces of several of the students we met earlier at the school. Looking past their smiles, I take in the reality of the environment surrounding me. It looks like the storage yard of a utility-sized manufacturing facility. As far as the eye can see, tubular concrete sections of sewer pipe lay on the ground, lined up in rows. The pipes lying on their side stand about six feet tall. Each one houses a family. Enterprising parents have devised ways to enclose each pipe, installing something of a flat floor. Some built brick walls on either end, leaving just enough room for a front door.

Each contains room for a stack of cots for sleeping. Tiny kitchens. Wood-burning stoves for cooking and for heat.

> I look inside one of the pipe houses and see two school uniforms hanging over a bed.

The children introduce us to moms and dads and siblings. More photos. More soccer. More laughter. I look inside one of the pipe houses and see two school uniforms hanging over a bed.

Back at the school, these kids seemed so much like their American counterparts. So much like my own children—eager to play, on the edge of mischief, yet willing to conform and please their teachers. But here, in Pipe Village, I see them in the context of their families. I remember the poster—"Do what you can, where you are, with what you have." And as I look around me, it isn't much. My own notion of what I have versus what I need is called to account.

Some of the students have both a mother and a father. Others live with extended family. Most of these discarded concrete pipes would have otherwise been installed in the more affluent part of town to provide drainage. For now, they are cold tubular walls that provide shelter to about 250

Dalits. Amid the starkness of the surroundings, we are told that Pipe Village would be a different place if not for the school.

There is not much time for reflection; the children want to play. Looking around, I can tell that our team is falling right in line with this vision thing. They are hooked on these Dalit kids; hooked on the hope that abounds in this place. I will have a hard time getting them back on the bus. Nevertheless, we drag ourselves away from these young stars and we depart.

Back on the bus, none of us wants to talk. We are taking it in. Processing. I see tears and hear sniffing behind me. Pipe Village got to us. Something powerful is stirring deep within us. It's clear to us all: I think we have just seen history in the making.

For the next few days, we travel from slum to dump site to schools. We talk to teachers and administrators and more students. We listen to their stories. We tour the slums. Every visit confirms

Pipe Village got to us. It's clear to us all: We have just seen history in the making.

what we saw the first day we arrived. It is more than sensory overload. It leaves us with just one thought: how lives are being radically transformed through the power of education brought to communities where, before, there was none.

After three long days of emotionally charged touring, I found myself in a new city, Bangalore, exhausted and ready to do nothing but drop into my single bed. Peering through the half-plastic, half-polyester curtain that shielded my window from the noise and poverty of the street below, I saw the red flashing of the neon sign displaying the hotel's name: the Corporate Stay. At that moment in time, it seemed like a witty play on words. Have I become the corporate man? Have I been yanked out of my nice corporate cocoon and brought face-to-face with what I think my people need? No, it's not just what *they* need, but what *I* need.

The bed is hard as a brick. Reminds me of the concrete sewer pipes. The television set with rabbit ears on top is blinking away at the foot of my bed. An Indian game show, flickering. Snowy distortion fuzzes it up. I hit the remote and turn it off. The room goes quiet.

I think of my incredible wife back home and our three children. I miss tucking them in. The regular story time. The giggles. The hugs. The endless, clever delay tactics. They don't want me to leave their room. I feel empty without them here. I look at their picture in my wallet. They smile back at me. I drift off to a welcome sleep.

A TIME TO WEEP

Suddenly, however, I am startled awake. It is perhaps three in the morning. I know I have had a disturbing, unsettling dream. But when I snap to consciousness, I have no recollection of the detail or the images. No sights. No sounds. No story. No people. I sit up. I am sobbing. Deep, heavy, repetitive sobs.

I have not wept like this in recent memory. I am glad to be alone in the room. It is a cry that comes from some distant place deep inside. I don't want it to stop. Rather than try to prevent it, I let it go.

I hear voices echoing:

"One dolla! Money money! Pleeze! Help me!"

A little boy taps at his lips.

"Dalits," explains my host.

"Your church is the largest congregation that has come to help us. You are from the most capable nation on the face of the earth."

"I want to be a doctor."

"I'm going to be a pastor" ". . . a policeman" ". . . a teacher" ". . . a lawyer."

"Our goal is one thousand schools."

"Money money! Pleeze! Help me!"

"Do what you can . . . where you are . . . with what you have."

"I think we have just seen history in the making."

So I let it go. I just lie back down and weep. My sobbing slips into a prayer. "OK, Lord. I don't understand all this. The money. The resources.

The schools. How do I explain this? How do I tell the story? How do I transfer the passion? The vision? This is not *my* vision. It is *Yours*. Your vision, Lord, has captured me."

I slip out from under my blanket and sheets, and do something I rarely do. I kneel down beside the hard bed at the Corporate Stay Hotel in Bangalore. I'm alone in my room. But not really. My face is wet.

"Lord God in heaven . . . I'll raise money. I'll talk to whoever will listen. I'll go to India . . . I'll go anywhere. These are not empty words coming from me now. This is what I am. This is *who* I am. I have been captured by what You have shown me."

I draw in a long, slow breath of Indian air. The room is dark. And still. I have only one more thing to say.

"Lord, I'm in. I am so in."

From that day to this, I have become a student of the movement that is transforming a nation.

Chapter 2

DECLARATION

I REMEMBER CLEARLY the day when I heard about the man whose work would provide the spark igniting the irrepressible movement toward "Global Freedom." His name is Udit Raj.

Udit Raj is a Dalit with a PhD.

After my encounter with the children in the schools of Hyderabad and Bangalore, after hearing their pleading for "one dolla" over and over, I was surprised to learn that not all of India's 250 million Dalits live in rank poverty. A few have broken free. Udit Raj is one of them. He was born in 1961 in a small hamlet called Ramnagar in the district (county) of Allahabad in the largest state in India, Uttar Pradesh.

His name has not always been Udit Raj.

Before I made my first visit, our church was committed to the freedom of Dalit children. My friend and colleague Jay Hoff had implemented our initial planning over several years. We had already built several schools. After my time with our team in Hyderabad, we were determined to increase our commitment and build more: two hundred in the next ten years. But I still had a lot to learn. The Dalit people and their plight fueled my motivation. I went after this knowledge with full force.

A whole new world opened up to me. Curiosity reawakened from somewhere deep inside. I could not stop the questions. I read books with a new sense of anticipation and intention. I kept notes; my journal entries proliferated. The story seemed like a giant puzzle I wanted to piece together. Some may well have accused me of obsession. It seemed more to me like a calling.

I heard that there had been a significant turning point in the movement toward Dalit Freedom. I knew that it happened on a cool, sunny November day in India's capital city, New Delhi, just a few years back, in 2001. I wanted to know more. The story that emerged in my research helped me understand just what it was that stoked the fire of Joseph's passion.

I imagined what it must have been like for people like Udit Raj and Joseph D'souza to grow up in India. I thought about those magical Indian jungles of the storybooks, home to every exotic animal associated with Indian lore. If I had been raised in India, I thought, I would have been like Rudyard Kipling's Mowgli, the young jungle boy in his classic children's story *The Jungle Book*, written in 1894. In those thick forests live the kind of wolves who raised Mowgli; here we meet panthers like Bagheera and tigers like Shere Khan (Kipling's timeless characters). There were pythons and monkeys and the Asian elephants and the great one-horned rhinoceros. Colorful birds and big-winged butterflies and creepy crawlers would have been part of my world as a boy. Tom Sawyer and Huck Finn had nothing compared to the rich adventures that I would have had.

These stories would have been *my* stories, if my imaginary childhood in India had been real. I would know the jungle. The tales of the mysterious, lush forest would have fascinated me as a boy.

ESCAPING THE "TIGER"

But this popular, romanticized, thoroughly British version of life in India shrouds a more accurate vision of life in India for a growing boy. I now know about another, more dangerous man-eating Tiger devouring people all over India. No one understands this better than Joseph D'souza's friend and colleague Udit Raj.

Born Ram Raj, the odds were stacked against him back in his village on the edge of town. He was a Dalit.

From the earliest days, he knew what that meant. His ebony skin bore undeniable testimony to his status: he was born an *untouchable.*

His father and mother worked hard. They took orders from the local upper-caste members of society, the Brahmins. Young Ram considered his parents' taskmasters to be mean and distant. It was their lot, his mother told him. Don't be bothered. Just accept it.

> The teacher assumed that as a Dalit, Ram would be responsible for the dirty, menial tasks. He took out the trash. He cleaned up after lunch.

A neighbor girl, a friend and playmate, simply disappeared one day. He later learned that her parents sold her to a stranger who had passed by. No one heard from her again. There were many stories like this.

School was optional in his town. No one cared if Ram showed up. And when he did, he was sent to the back of the class, where untouchables are expected to sit. The teacher assumed that as a Dalit, he would be responsible for the dirty, menial tasks. He took out the trash. He cleaned up after lunch, a meal he often had to skip because he had no food from home. But in spite of his status, his teachers liked him. He had the kind of hunger for knowledge that every teacher hopes to find in a student. Some of them secretly tutored him as teachers do with a self-motivated, eager learner.

Ram was an exceptional child, curious and cunning. He learned to read early by sheer determination. But he also had a quick temper. Whenever he witnessed abuse, he came to the defense of the abused. It sometimes got him into trouble. He was smart. He was also self-reliant. Some labeled him an agitator, a firebrand, even before he knew anything about caste laws.

In the village, he felt the stares. His part of the neighborhood had no access to water. There were no utilities. When the power lines came to town, they were routed away from his section of the village. His mother and father barely made enough money for food. Young Ram knew that the high-caste local Hindu priest was in charge. However, neither his parents nor he could ever approach the man to petition for change.

> Even his shadow would be desecrated if it accidentally crossed over the body of an upper-caste Hindu.

He had been taught to keep his distance. Even his shadow would be desecrated if it accidentally crossed over the body of an upper-caste Hindu. There would be a heavy price to pay for drifting over the boundary lines. He could not sip from the same cup, walk the same trails, or climb the same trees. He was untouchable because of a supposed dark transgression committed in a former life. He must accept this. To question the rules is bad karma. So over the evening campfires, his grandfather and his father and his neighbors taught the boy lessons of life as it is.

Know your station and keep it. That was rule number one.

He tried to observe the traditions and customs of the village, but questioned the seemingly strange rituals, from weddings to births to funerals to holidays to festivals. His mother and father discouraged his questions; any feeble answers they offered did not satisfy him.

He witnessed the terror in the eyes of his neighbors if a cow happened to be killed. The guilty party would be charged with the crime and then banished from the village. The alleged perpetrator would be forced to eat cow dung as a purification rite to atone for his sin. None of this made any sense to the young boy. He considered it a terrible bondage, even before he knew the word.

He managed by pure grit to get himself into an English-speaking school. He read every book he could find and lost himself in the pages. He loved adventure stories. He played cricket with his Dalit pals. He would sneak around the neighborhood to watch and listen to television sets. His English improved.

He persevered and advanced through the toughest courses, emerging as an intelligent, articulate, ambitious learner. He wrote with depth and insight; he spoke with passion and charm. His smile lit up the room. He was a fun-loving prankster.

Ram managed to pass his series of tests and won admittance to the University at Allahabad. He met some professors and administrators who believed privately that the caste system was an abomination. They helped him navigate the campus and the course load. The university was built in 1887 during the British colonial period. A liberal arts college, it was founded on the classics of liberal education. For the first time in his life, he was treated (for the most part) as an equal. In the university environment, caste distinctions were minimized. He had full access to the library. His professors took an interest in his progress. He got involved in social causes.

But prejudice could be found even in the liberal university setting. The few Dalits who gained entrance were often belittled, discounted, and ridiculed. Ram came to the defense of a fellow student, also a Dalit, and a fight broke out. Fists flew. It attracted a large crowd. The old Hindu prejudices were reawakened. It triggered a memorable series of protests on campus that divided the student body. Ram's passions were inflamed. The incident changed him forever.

THE DREAM OF A NEW INDIA

The conflicts he battled in childhood came into focus. He tasted freedom far from the caste-based constraints of his hometown. But he understood better now. In this new world he felt the old oppression, abuse, and exploitation renewed as he had back in the village, where he watched his parents and his neighbors accept a life of hardship, deprivation, and cruelty.

It set him on an academic quest. He studied some of the great liberation movements of history. He learned about Gandhi and Ambedkar, the architect of India's constitution, and about the struggle for independence from Great Britain and the creation of the world's largest democracy. He read books about the economic exploitation of natural and human resources. He studied the culture and traditions of his own Hindu religion: a system of hierarchical castes, casteism. He learned about the inbred concept of *untouchability*. He took courses on comparative religion and learned about alternate worldviews rooted in Christianity, Islam, Judaism, Buddhism, Zoroastrianism, and the many strains of his own Hinduism.

He learned about the clash between capitalism and socialism, about Marx and Mao, about the sweeping epic historical drama of two World Wars in his own century. He studied the Civil War in America and the Emancipation Proclamation penned by Abraham Lincoln. He read about the abolitionist tradition, from Wilberforce in England to the Quakers of New England. He learned about apartheid in South Africa and the irrepressible courage of Nelson Mandela. He read the speeches and sermons of Martin Luther King Jr. and pondered the meaning and the risks of civil disobedience. He studied Malcolm X and his debate with King over nonviolent protest. He read biographies of Mahatma Gandhi: his years as a law student at University College in London, his travels to South Africa and encounter with apartheid, his battle to mobilize the nation against British rule, his assassination by a Hindu radical, his attitudes toward untouchables. Ram focused on Dr. B. R. Ambedkar's argument with Gandhi, and how this unlikely scholar was selected to craft the immortal lines of India's new constitution. He couldn't get enough. He had questions for everyone.

He understood that his home country, the emerging nation of India, with over a billion people, was on the verge of becoming a world power. He wanted to be a part. He dreamed big dreams.

And that's when he met Seema, an upper-class (Khatri) student who would have never considered spending the span of her adult life married to a Dalit. But Ram Raj had something that made him stand out from all the rest. He later described their relationship: "I am very dark, almost black, but my wife is as fair as an Englishwoman, and I must say that although ours was a love marriage in which her intrinsic qualities mattered more than looks, I found her very attractive."

Theirs would not be a traditional Hindu-arranged marriage. He used every power of persuasion to convince her to take his hand, without parental consent. She accepted his proposal.

And in the process, he separated himself from traditions woven into the cultural convention of his homeland. His parents predicted disaster. It was bad karma. His ambitions would destroy him, they said. Her parents believed they had lost a daughter. But Ram and Seema were deliriously happy and eager to make a life.

Ram was now a college graduate with high marks, a beautiful wife, and high ambition. He landed a coveted government job with the India Revenue Service (IRS) and quickly moved up the ranks all the way to District Commissioner in New Delhi. Along the way, he picked up graduate degrees, including a doctorate.

He had come a long way from that remote village to the capital city of India, now a respected high-ranking government official responsible for the oversight of a large staff whose mission was to collect taxes. From all outward appearances, Ram Raj had arrived. He had a career, a beautiful family, a home, position, and the admiration of the community.

A MARCH OF MILLIONS

But something dark haunted him. His people continued to suffer. Time after time, he encountered not-so-subtle discrimination. Even though he and Seema enjoyed a relatively comfortable lifestyle with their two children, Ram Raj knew he was an exception. The rule kept most of his fellow Dalits, 250 million of them, in a state of perpetual misuse. While he enjoyed a good, prosperous life, his family back in the village of Ramnagar was exploited. Seema's parents were embarrassed. No success, no promotion, no recognition from the government could erase his wife's parents' humiliation. Their grandchildren had a Dalit for a father. Their daughter had a Dalit for a husband. They could not let Ram or Seema forget.

There was no escaping his identity. He was a Dalit.

Ram understood: this discrimination was systemic, ancient, culturally ingrained, and religiously sanctioned. Legislation could not change those realities. But it gnawed away at his sense of self. He wanted more for his own children.

That's when it came to him: the idea of a Million Man March on New Delhi.

He read about the 1963 March on Washington when Martin Luther King stood on the steps of the Lincoln Memorial and declared, "I have a dream." He followed the history. Five years after that famous speech, in 1968 King led the Poor People's Campaign that filled the Washington Mall again, garnering the attention of the global media. Raj also followed the rise of Louis Farrakhan (the supreme minister of the Nation of Islam in America), who mobilized the Million Man March of 1995, also in Washington DC, forcing an unwilling nation to face issues of racism, economic inequities, and damaged self-esteem, particularly for African-American males. Then, two years later, in 1997 the Promise Keepers drew a million men or more to celebrate their Christian commitment.

But none of that compared to his fascination with the legendary Dalit, Bhimrao Ramji (B. R.) Ambedkar. Ram and Seema would talk about him late into the night, reflecting on his legacy.

Dr. B. R. Ambedkar is renowned as the "Chief Architect of the Indian Constitution" and "The Thomas Jefferson of India." He was born in 1891 an "untouchable." A Dalit. He spent his entire life battling the Hindu caste system of *Chaturvarna*, which categorizes all of Hindu society into four classes. After fighting that system all his life as an untouchable, he believed that the only solution for India's Dalits was conversion from Hinduism to, in his case, Buddhism. Ambedkar understood that such a conversion would be illegal. But it became his passion.

Like Gandhi, Ambedkar took his undergraduate studies in the United Kingdom. He also studied in the United States. He was a graduate of Columbia University and the London School of Economics. Ram Raj considered Ambedkar a hero. He parlayed his status as an untouchable into the history books as a national leader in his beloved India. He battled for the rights of untouchables to have access to water, education, and Hindu temples. He publicly argued with Mahatma Gandhi for his failure to address the problems of untouchability when he had the opportunity. Gandhi's approach was "separate but equal." That was not enough. Ambedkar considered the Mahatma a victim of compromise.

Gandhi was wrong, declared Ambedkar. Gandhi's failure to denounce Hinduism for its systemic, fundamental, irreversible, and cruel oppression of nearly one-third of India's population was inexcusable. Ambedkar took Gandhi's revolution a giant step forward. In 1956, Ambedkar officially and ceremoniously ignored convention and outmoded laws when he publicly converted from Hinduism to Buddhism in a very visible act of civil disobedience. That same year, in a public mass conversion, five hundred thousand Dalits followed his example. Together, they renounced Hinduism in a specific indictment, listing Hinduism's offense in Twenty-Two Vows recited en masse for the world to hear. The architect of India's first democratic constitution, Dr. B. R. Ambedkar, penned those affirmations.

The time was right. Dalit oppression must end once and for all.

Ram Raj studied all twenty-two vows. They were powerful and liberating, he thought.

The time was right. Dalit oppression must end once and for all. The world must know. The Hindu caste system must be eradicated. Ram Raj picked up the torch where Ambedkar had left off. Seema supported him. He would reawaken all of India and the whole world to the passions of B. R. Ambedkar. He could hardly sleep.

There was only one problem. The conversion he wanted to pursue was still, as in the days of Ambedkar, illegal. It was an obstacle he would have to navigate.

To this day, eight of India's twenty-eight states enforce anticonversion laws. These vary state by state, but the intent is clear: it is a criminal violation of the code of law for a Dalit to convert from Hinduism. There is no freedom of religion. In some cases, the law requires a person to report his or her conversion to a government official. To fail to do so is a criminal offense punishable with prison time. Some of the laws ban conversion away *from* Hinduism outright, but allow for conversion *to* Hinduism. These laws are a carryover from a tradition embedded in the collective culture of an entire nation for three thousand years.

Ambedkar, as an untouchable, understood the full implication. While most states eliminated these archaic laws from their official books, eight continued to impose this debilitating restriction on their citizens. To this day, Dalits are prohibited from access to the temple. Brahmins, who provide guidance and counsel and support to the community, may have no contact with untouchables. Dalits are considered hopelessly contaminated, at least in this life. Everything they touch is infected; they are banned to a life of social quarantine, remaining isolated and cut off from the social order. Ambedkar found these ideas to be an absurd abomination, a blight on the high culture and nobility of Indian society. He dedicated his life to the eradication of not only the code but the prevailing attitude that accommodated, even welcomed these laws.

Ram Raj fully embraced Ambedkar's vision. He planned to do something about it.

DANGER AHEAD

As I learned more about the scope of the problem of Dalit discrimination, and captured something of the passions of Ram Raj as a social reformer, Dr. D'souza's focus became mine. While Ram Raj and I have differing views on many things, I came to appreciate his determination. His journey teaches me so much. I understand and respect Dr. D'souza for building this strategic friendship with a man who is such a catalyst for the emancipation of his people.

I continued my research. This was a key turning point in modern-day Dalit history. Ram Raj would put his dream on the national stage.

The target date was set: November 4, 2001. Raj secured a permit in New Delhi, choosing a venue with enough open space to accommodate an audience of one million Dalits. For nearly three years, he mapped out his plan. It would be a spectacular political and social statement that would capture the attention of the national and international media. A global event. The time was right.

He raised money. He shared his vision. He put together a team of organizers. He blitzed the media. He tapped into the existing organizations and leaders who understood the problems of untouchability. They came from the academic, religious, and social worlds. Authors and lecturers, social activists, religious leaders, politicians, philosophers, artists, musicians, business leaders, historians representing all the traditions—all of them would be recruited to join in the event.

It would be an Emancipation Proclamation in the tradition of Abraham Lincoln, almost 150 years earlier on the other side of the globe. Ram would unearth Ambedkar's Twenty-Two Vows. They would be republished, repeated en masse. It would be a frontal assault on a social evil. But in the tradition of Gandhi and King, it would be nonviolent.

He shared his dream. He knew the risk of violence. The risk of civil war, the risk of retaliation was real. Everyone understood. But it was time to open the debate. It was time for liberation from fear, from hunger, from oppression, from separation and from injustice.

Ram Raj—Dalit, scholar, husband, father, government official, student of history, social activist, disciple of Ambedkar—was ready.

The word got out.

In the initial planning stage, expanding on Ambedkar's model, he cultivated relationships and intended to include representatives from all the major religious groups: Christianity, Islam, and Buddhism. Ram was not as concerned about what religion the liberated Dalit might choose. He also worked to guarantee that the Dalits would *have* a choice. In the choosing, all persons might affirm their own standing and have a role in determining their own destiny.

As Raj promoted the November 2001 event, enthusiasm accelerated. In the Christian community, news of the mass gathering circled the globe through mission agencies in a flash. He flew to the United States and met with several Christian groups with a known interest in India. He also arranged a series of meetings in India with numerous religious leaders and their constituencies. He took a leave of absence from his position at the India Revenue Service. His own organization, The All India Confederation of Scheduled Castes/Scheduled Tribes Organizations, became the fund-raising and organizing group for the most ambitious event ever planned in the name of Dalit Freedom—the gathering of one million Dalits in the nation's capital at the Ram Lila Grounds in New Delhi. It was the very place President Eisenhower appeared on December 13, 1959, and said, "We believe that freedom ultimately will be won everywhere."

The stated purpose for the mass meeting was twofold. First, he wanted to declare Dalit independence from the shackles of the Hindu religion by renouncing its iron-gripped hold. Second, Raj would invite the newly freed Dalits to embrace one of the great religions: Christianity, Islam, or Buddhism. It would be a direct challenge to what he called a "decadent social order," which stands steadfastly against conversion.

His careful planning and spot-on strategy development, however, could not prevent the two unscheduled global developments, which would, in the final days of planning, alter the course of the historic event in unexpected ways. First: reprisals triggered by an over-enthusiastic American Christian community. Second: the events of September 11, 2001—known forever as "9/11."

News of Ram Raj's plans spread through the Christian world like an October Southern California brush fire fueled by the Santa Ana winds. Raj openly shared his vision of renouncing Hinduism in the tradition of Dr. B. R. Ambedkar. He spoke of presenting the 250 million Dalits with the alternatives of other religions, including Christianity. He contacted several high-profile evangelists seeking their support. He invited some of them to participate in the event.

> Joseph D'souza and his colleagues understood the nuanced strategies of evangelism in a country that makes conversion illegal.

Joseph D'souza and his colleagues understood the nuanced strategies of evangelism in a country that makes conversion illegal. It is not a simple thing. Christians have sought to share the good news for hundreds of years. The Gospel message by definition demands a response. But in a nation predisposed to reject that message, where violence can be and all too often is the means by which that message is silenced, thoughtful Christians have learned to navigate through the minefields with sensitivity, caution, and wisdom. But not all well-meaning Christians comprehend the dangers.

Prayer alerts were trumpeted all over the world through Christian media outlets, including radio and television. Claims of potential Christian conversions in the tens of thousands, perhaps millions, were projected. Raj's New Delhi event was portrayed as a mass evangelistic crusade. Many mission agencies dropped other plans and strategized to seize the opportunity. Portable baptism tents were designed and funded, and construction initiated. Tens of thousands of Bibles were printed in the predominant language of Hindi. Religious books targeted at the Dalit population also hit the printing presses. Agencies recruited short-term missionaries, evangelists, and church planters and planned to descend on New Delhi on November 4, prepared to meet with an inestimable number of new converts. Though not a committed Christian, but still a seeker, Raj was hailed as a modern-day apostle, ushering in a massive, unprecedented influx of new believers to the Christian fold.

Soon, the Vishwa Hindu Parishad (VHP), the radical Hindu fundamentalist sect, learned of the international plans. It was all they needed. They protested that foreign agitators were planning to invade the country with the express purpose of disrupting the peace and upsetting the social order. They immediately demanded that the district commissioner of police in New Delhi shut down the event and revoke Ram's permit. They presented the Christian promotional materials as hard evidence. The VHP has a long history of bloody violence. According to one report, "Extremist Hindus threatened a bloodbath if the rally took place."

The pressure was on. Ram Raj consulted with his advisors. He called in trusted Christian leaders, including Dr. D'souza. The threat was real. If outside Christians showed up in great numbers with baptismal tents and counselors and literature and an army of trainers, the results could well be catastrophic.

Then, a mere fifty-four days before the scheduled gathering in New Delhi, the surprise terrorist attacks on America, on September 11, 2001, added to the drama.

On the surface, this tragic episode seems entirely unrelated to the planned event in New Delhi. But the timing of the drama is notable. The disaster dominated global media weeks before the planned gathering of a million Dalits. The massive destruction and cold-blooded killing of thousands of innocent American citizens put the entire world on high alert. Global war seemed a distinct possibility. Radical terrorists felt empowered. The global economic engine came to an abrupt halt and remained in a state of paralysis.

The crisis was felt everywhere, including the law enforcement offices of New Delhi and in the planning centers of the All India Confederation of Scheduled Castes/Scheduled Tribes Organizations. Ram and his committee recognized that the focus on both Christianity and Islam were perilous flashpoints. A pragmatist, Raj called off conversions to both Christianity and Islam. The event would limit the ceremony to the less threatening *diksha*: a Buddhist conversion.

Hinduism's conservative leadership considers conversion to Christianity or Islam to be a direct affront to the Indian social order. It is grounds for denial of the rights of citizenship. Not so in the case of Buddhism. The Vedas (the Hindu scripture) recognizes the Buddha as the ninth Avatar of Vishnu; that is, the Krishna (the same Krishna as in Buddhism) is the ninth incarnation of the supreme deity. A Hindu, technically, cannot deny a turn to Buddhism. On this basis, Ram Raj promoted this event as a "reaffirmation," and as such, could not be prohibited on the grounds of "illegal conversion" by government officials. He effectively took away their excuse for closing him down.

Many of the Christians who had anticipated the event expressed their deep disappointment. Some believed they had been misled. Certainly, there were those in the Islamic community who felt the same.

Raj had fought for years to make this event an undeniable statement that casteism must be eradicated from India in all its destructive forms. He put everything he had on the line. His primary hero, B. R. Ambedkar, did not even attempt to include Christians or Muslims in his efforts to break the back of anticonversion laws. Raj had. He had convened multireligious gatherings in the past, with significant results. There was a surprising and gratifying solidarity among all those who joined forces to battle casteism.

But there were also great risks.

In the final days before the event, as predicted by many of Raj's critics,

New Delhi's District Commissioner of the Police, R. S. Krishnaia, pulled the permit. As far as the city was concerned, the event was over.

But Ram Raj would not be denied. His hero, B. R. Ambedkar, faced terrible opposition, but he did not back down. His friend Dr. Joseph D'souza, stood with him in the fight.

Raj was vilified in New Delhi's newspapers and radio broadcasts. They challenged his credentials. They misrepresented his motives. The police went on full alert to turn back the hundreds of thousands of Dalits pouring into New Delhi. They posted billboards and signs all over the city: "Dalit Gathering CANCELLED."

> The police went on full alert to turn back the hundreds of thousands of Dalits pouring into New Delhi.

The police force watched highways for buses and vans carrying Dalits into the city. They were pulled over and turned back. Vigilante gangs from a coordinated VHP (the radical Hindu fundamentalists) intimidated and threatened Dalits moving toward the center of town. The VHP and RSS (Rashtriya Swayamsevak Sangh) and BJP (Bharatiya Janata Party) along with Bajrang Dal (the youth wing of the VHP) all produced inflammatory materials. They explained with convoluted logic that the proposed conversion ceremony, even though it was limited to Buddhism, was a Western Christian conspiracy to undermine Indian Hindu culture. Bearing arms, along with the police force, the vigilantes bullied and coerced, turning many away. They stormed bus and train stations, confronting people fitting the Dalit profile. The Dalits were told to go back home. Many did.

In a charged atmosphere of fear and intimidation, with intense pressure from all around, Ram Raj rallied to counter the government's "dictatorial" action. He filed an immediate appeal to K. R. Narayanan, then-president of India. He complained that the government had no authority to cancel a *diksha*. The constitution guaranteed religious freedom, and the president was sworn to uphold it. Foreign dignitaries were in New Delhi for the event. Thousands of Dalits had already gathered. Raj complained that some 350 thousand Dalits had been improperly detained. It was an embarrassment to the democratic ideals of the Indian government.

Fear of confrontation mounted. Ram continued to preach nonviolence. One of his Dalit leaders proclaimed, "If, as the police fear, violence breaks out, it will be the responsibility of the government. If the police shoot, we will take the bullets."

The event went ahead, but not at the Ram Lila Grounds. Police stood armed at the entrances of that large facility and told arriving folks that there was no event. Banners made the point. But the president yielded, and at the last possible moment, approved a permit at an alternate site— the smaller grounds at Ambedkar Bhavan (named for Raj's hero).

By this time, most of the anticipated one million participants had been blocked, distracted, or otherwise prevented from participating. The gathering was the talk of New Delhi and all of India. Even so, while accounts vary, between fifty and one hundred thousand crowded onto the grounds for the watershed event.

My friend Joseph D'souza was there.

In a bulletproof vest.

Chapter 3

RELEASE AND RESTORATION

April 2003 to February 2004—California

JUST AS THERE WAS A moment in my life when vision captured me, there was also a moment in my life when vision escaped me. That night in Bangalore, everything changed. Up until then, all my life I had been grasping—I understand now—for the wrong stuff.

People who know me well will tell you I have always had great expectations. When I picked up a trumpet, I wanted to play with the best. And I did. I set out to serve God. My models for ministry were some of the nation's most influential people. My first real mentor in pastoral ministry led the largest church in our denomination. He took me in; promoted me up the ranks. We shared big dreams.

My parents surrounded me with love and support and affirmation. My big brothers, Michael and Mark, set the pace. The thought of failure never really occurred to me. Then, on one fateful Monday afternoon, the bottom fell out.

WHEN OUR CHURCH ALMOST DIED

Our church has had a reputation for growth since the beginning, one hundred years ago. It has always been an accepting, affirming place where people feel comfortable, open. That's not to say that we have watered down the message. We hold on to the conviction that people need to cultivate their spiritual life. We stand on a firm foundation. There is forgiveness and wholeness available to anyone who will be open to God's message of healing and hope. The Gospel is good news.

> To understand the power of the vision of what became the Global Freedom movement, you need to understand how close we came to total disaster.

That's how our church became our denomination's fastest-growing, largest congregation in the United States.

It is important for me to tell you the story of the near-extinction of this great church. But it will be challenging because when things go wrong, one of our first instincts is to assess blame. Identifying fault is a way of life in our culture. If there is an airplane crash, we send in the National Transportation Safety Board to do a thorough, independent investigation to determine precisely what happened and who is to blame. There are millions of dollars of damage at stake. Someone will pay. Who will it be?

It also happens in churches. It is impossible to measure the damage inflicted on the kingdom of God through the ages by so-called believers who missed it. There is plenty of blame to go around. As I tell the story of our church, understand this—it will be *my* version. So let me say it at the outset, as clearly as I can: I share in the blame.

To understand the power of the vision of what we have termed the Global Freedom movement, you need to understand how close we came to total disaster. I have come to believe that we are in a life-and-death struggle to plant the flag of justice. Reconciliation is never easy. When we get serious about discipleship, there will be a price to pay.

I also believe firmly that the rewards far outweigh the cost.

Our church walked through its own valley of the shadow of death. It was more than bad. We worked so painfully hard to prevent it, but it happened anyway. A church of well over four thousand came within a hair's breadth of collapse just as a major building project was halfway completed.

After fourteen years of leadership that brought me to the role of executive pastor in a church of over ninety full-time paid staff, in a matter of a few dreadful minutes, I found myself unemployed.

Whatever vision I had up until that day vanished. Whatever hopes and dreams I had for our church evaporated. My carefully laid plans for my family were suspended. The foundations shook. It was a dizzying disorientation that I had never before experienced.

The seeds of destruction are just beneath the soil of every organization. With a little watering and feeding, those seeds germinate and shoot through the surface. With tender care, pruning, and shaping, those tiny seeds mature. The vines twist together and bear their poisonous fruit.

Somehow, I believed we were exempt. We had the commitment and the tools to recognize those shoots for what they were: weeds. And I thought we did a pretty good job of rooting them out.

But I was wrong.

Our church comes from a long tradition of solid commitments. Certain core convictions bind us together. We believe in the authority of the Bible. We promote a personal relationship with the living God. We affirm the experience of conversion. We embrace the redeeming work of Jesus. We condemn the abuses of the church throughout the centuries and propose a new and fresh way of understanding godliness.

And from the earliest days, we have embraced the conviction that the Gospel has social implications. Trace it back all the way, and you will find our forebears active in the abolitionist movement. We take seriously Jesus' instruction to tend to the needs of the disenfranchised.

I love *the* church. (The church is the universal collection of believers in Christ throughout the world and through the corridors of time.) I love *our* church. I have seen too much of God's work to think otherwise. Marriages restored. Families healed. Businesses nurtured. Educations completed. Athletes motivated. Musicians launched. Hospitals built. Hungry fed. Books written and read. Worship transporting people into the presence of God. Grandparents buried and memorialized. Grief comforted. Anger silenced. Animosities reconciled. Children taught. Hope restored. Wounds treated. Generosity abounding. Communities affirmed. Crises become purpose. Forgiveness reigns. Mercy flows. Grace dispensed. It is all there. I revel in the shepherding role. It fills me with a joy that energizes me.

> Three battlefields too often cripple the church: worship, governance, purpose.

So when things go wrong, and all those grand purposes become threatened, it is a tragedy of the first rank. And that's what happened.

I wish I could explain where it all began, but I can't. Upon reflection, particularly in those painful days when I no longer had a job, I identified some of the seeds of destruction that were planted in our vineyard. I am convinced that these seeds are not unique to us. In fact, I believe they have already done considerable damage to our movement.

They have effectively silenced too many of my colleagues in pastoral ministry. They have prompted too many believers to abandon our precious faith. They have handed a new breed of outspoken atheists (who profit by publishing accounts of the missteps and misdeeds of the so-called faithful) a silver platter filled with evidence for their cause.

Three battlefields too often cripple the church: worship, governance, purpose. The debates over how we worship, how leaders lead, why we exist may not only distract but derail ministry. I believed for a long time that we at our church had found a healthy balance in these arenas. I believed it was the basis of our growth. But nearly thirteen years into my ministry, I found out I was wrong.

"NO LONGER ON THE SAME PAGE"

During my tenure as associate pastor, our growth, I suppose you could say, was nothing short of spectacular. It had little to do with me. Our leadership team worked well together. We were seeing results, adding staff, winning national acclaim for our children's programs. Our youth initiatives yielded high-energy impact on our local high schools and beyond. Our men came together as a band of brothers and impacted hundreds of other men. Families joined together with new purpose and joy. Businesses benefited from leaders with a new commitment to integrity.

However, what we failed to recognize was that we had grown so large, so fast, that we had also outgrown our competencies. We did not recognize the seriousness of the battles simmering right beneath the surface. We were in denial.

I was the second in command in what clearly had become a hierarchical organization. My boss, who was also my mentor, my coach, and at one time, my hero, succumbed as I did to the church debates that nearly shattered everything we had worked so hard to build.

As time passed, we became adversaries. And I remained blissfully unaware.

It was Easter Sunday. We exchanged an easy greeting. I congratulated him on a terrific sermon. It was a genuine remark. He thanked me, and then asked if I would stop by his house the following day.

"Sure," I said.

"Good. Make it 1:30."

It was nothing unusual. We met often. There was always plenty to talk about. Our staff had expanded tremendously. Easter remains the highlight of the year for us.

The next day after a round of golf, I knocked on the door at the appointed time. It surprised me to see several other cars in the driveway. I recognized some of them. I wondered for a moment if I'd missed the agenda. I shrugged, realizing that the elders frequently met with us unannounced, and I walked in.

I noticed an air of tension in the room. The greetings were warm, but there was an edge. I took a deep breath and sat down on a comfortable, overstuffed chair. I grabbed my bottle of water. I took a sip and twisted the top back in place.

My superior turned to me with an odd, unexpected look on his face. My heartbeat picked up its pace. I felt a new level of focus come to my spirit. I sat up in the chair.

"Matthew." He took a breath. "We are here to ask for your resignation."

I blinked. My eyes widened. "Excuse me?"

I turned to the others, friends I had known for years. These were the guys who welcomed me as a young pastor fresh out of school. They nurtured me through the expansion of my responsibilities. I traveled with them. Our families dined together. We had spent countless hours praying together. I viewed them as counselors, advisors, and encouragers. Now I looked at them, stunned by the announcement, and looked for confirmation.

Scanning the room, I glanced at each of them, one by one, as they sat motionless. They were, I could tell, in turmoil.

It was that surreal sense that you are not really in the room; that this is a dream or a movie scene or a theatrical performance on some imaginary stage. And as I took in more oxygen to feed the demands of that accelerating heartbeat, it all got hold of me.

My long tenure as a pastor in the church I loved was about to end. Abruptly.

My mind raced through all the issues of the church debates. I knew I had taken a stand. I had strong convictions about balancing biblical ministry and contemporary culture. I believed I had been loyal. I wanted to know why.

The explanation? We "were no longer on the same page." On one level, I understood. The worship thing. The governance thing. The purpose thing. Yes, we had differing perspectives. Indeed, we had differing approaches. Yes, our gift mix was different. Different, yes. Contradictory, no. Up until now, I called it complementary, not inconsistent. Diversity is good, I said. Variance, OK. But antagonism, no way. *Incompatibility*—a chance.

The inner conversation swirled just beneath my stunned silence. My questions nearly blinded me as I sat in that living room the day after Easter. But in my state of astonishment, I nodded in acquiescence. I had long ago come to respect these men who sat before me and submit to their judgments. I had such respect for them, I had nowhere to go but acceptance. Inwardly, however, I felt as if my professional and ministry life at this church I so dearly loved had just dropped off a cliff.

> The inner conversation swirled just beneath my stunned silence as I sat in that living room the day after Easter.

I had no plans for the immediate future. I knew the public explanations I was asked to give fell considerably short of complete accuracy. Soon, questions about honesty and integrity went out of control in a rumor mill only possible when it involves thousands who have been deprived of all the facts. Our congregation grouped together in huddles, trying to sort out fact from fiction; our young people rolled their eyes in disgust; and our staff wondered about job security.

I had often quoted the familiar maxim from the book of Proverbs: "Where there is no vision, the people perish." I have no better way of describing what happened to me than to say that I felt like I was perishing. My vision of what could be vanished. Something of great value, well, it left me.

Vision unites people, I often heard and read. But now, it seemed to me that vision drove good people apart.

To this day, I do not know how I explained all this to Mardi. I was confused. I was hurt. It was a kind of pain I had never experienced before. There was an emptiness. A hollowness. A creeping mistrust. All the dreams I had for my church, my family, my career—they were all gone.

Suddenly, I had time to think. No office to go to. No staff clamoring for appointments or answers to questions. Up until this moment, it is crazy how often I would hear, "Hey, Matthew . . . just the guy I was looking for!"

But now, they were not looking for me. They were moving on. Someone else made all those decisions. Someone else answered all those calls. Someone else waded through the emails.

Others offered advice.

They told me I should "experience joy in the time of crisis because of all the good things that will come out of it." I felt no joy.

They told me I would learn great lessons that would prepare me for something bigger and better. I had no interest in lessons. They told me that all great men and women know failure as well as victory. I hated the notion of failure. They told me it would be all right. I didn't say anything. But there was nothing in me that agreed.

Brokenness is part of God's plan for real healing, someone else said. That didn't help, either.

So I walked alone. I stood on a bluff one day overlooking the blue expanse of the Pacific Ocean and there, with the wind in my face, I wept.

When you are in free fall and every risk you have ever taken comes together at the same time and planet Earth is coming at you with the relentless speed of gravity, you pray.

For a couple of weeks, I felt that way. Everything I cared about disappeared. They told me that my office was no longer available to me. No more desk. No more voice mail. My assistant was reassigned. My email address—canceled. The hard drive—wiped clean. My routines stopped cold. My identity passed into oblivion. My replacement was announced. The relationships that sustained me and gave me purpose and joy were cut off.

I didn't know what else to do but pray. My prayers were not the garden-variety Sunday morning petitions for the sick. I had some serious questions for God.

The church was my life. I considered it my calling. A stewardship. We had serious momentum. My calendar was filled with plans for that summer and the fall ahead. The teams were in full gear. The building project moved forward—work crews making progress every day. We had designed the new facility to be a giant leap forward to provide a high-impact place for the community to engage in transformational activity. It would be a full-on media center capable of state-of-the-art programming. We were attracting some of the finest talent in the region to take it all to a new level of excellence. It had been years in the planning, with a celebration every time we jumped a hurdle or broke down a barrier or hit a target. There were so many confirmations. Up until that time, my calendar was marked with one victory after another. We held the firm conviction that God was the Master Designer of all those plans.

> I believed that I was called to be a pastor. Perhaps I had presumed. I asked God to explain.

And now it all appeared to be disintegrating before our very eyes. It was as though I'd been ejected out the door of a plane and I was falling fast, desperate to find the ripcord.

I believed that I was called to be a pastor. But now that conviction wavered. I wondered if I had missed it. Perhaps I had presumed. I asked God to explain.

I tested one theory: that all this meant that I ought to be somewhere else. The phone rang. Inquiries came in. Next thing I knew, I was putting together a résumé and sitting down for interviews. It felt so strange, really, to be in the presence of good people in different ministry contexts and considering the possibility that all this was essentially a call to go somewhere else.

I tested another theory: that perhaps pastoral ministry was not my calling after all. Some good people opened doors in the secular world of business. These opportunities came in during those heady days before the Great Recession and what has been called a global economic crisis.

What appeared to be a boundless expansion was still moving forward. The possibilities seemed to be limitless. I looked at the lifestyle of some of the people inviting me into their world and for a time, frankly, I thought it looked pretty good. Several of those interviews turned into offers. Mardi and I labored over the options.

I cannot really describe the turmoil I felt that summer. Despite the options laid before me, sadness and grief over my loss overwhelmed me. At the same time, my commitment to the vision of impacting North County for the kingdom of God with a high-energy, aggressive missional strategy had an equal, powerful grip on me.

But yet one more option was brewing.

A PLACE TO SOAR

While I was on staff back at the church that released me, I had a team working toward a clear vision. They told me that the vision I had articulated back then is what brought them to church. They wanted to keep that vision alive. They encouraged me to continue as a pastor, and to launch a new church based on the model we had pursued together with a whole heart. To hear them talk about it got me thinking and, I must admit, energized me.

John Erwin, along with several other longtime staff, was also dismissed just one week after I was released. John came to our church from the Midwest largely because he shared our vision. We began an intense conversation. In light of the proposal from a significant collection of good friends and supporters, John and I brainstormed together. We imagined a new church, committed to that vision and those values we talked about when he made his decision to sell his home after fourteen years in Minnesota and bring his family back to California just eight months prior.

Two other former staffers joined us in the conversation: one a top-flight administrator, the other an events planner. We spent countless hours dreaming of a church that would meet the real needs of real people. It would be a church for folks who are not comfortable in traditional church. It would be a place for artists to soar; a place where folks hungry for meaning and purpose would find it.

As word filtered out, supporters rallied behind us. To our amazement, contributions came in; enough to sustain us after the severance ran out. That October, we scheduled a meeting in the next town over, in the auditorium of a successful and growing credit union.

To my amazement, 450 people appeared. There were not enough chairs. They stood on the periphery and along the back wall. We prepared an up-tempo video to set the pace. John presented his version of our plans to penetrate North County with solid biblical teaching, community groups, and events that would target real needs. We would focus on children, making church both informative and fun. I shared from my heart. We would have a team approach to leadership. We would have an outward focus, not inward, expressing our burden for broken families and lost people who need a living relationship with a living God. Worship and the arts would contribute a great deal to our church's culture; we would utilize the best people we would find. I mapped it all out. We already had a formidable crew at the ready. I did my best to paint the picture verbally in living color.

The response of enthusiasm overwhelmed me. We took an offering. We asked people to let us know if they supported the vision. When we got the count, we knew we had what we needed. And more.

We called our new church The River. We liked the name because it calls up Jesus' metaphor: *rivers of living water*. We think people are looking for fresh water. It is basic to our survival as human beings. And it is essential to sustain our spirits, too.

Our gathering gave us the assurance that we were onto something significant. Our team gathered the following morning. There was excitement and energy in that room I will never forget.

I came home after the meeting and told Mardi. She saw a confidence in me that she had hoped and prayed that she would see again. I informed her straight-out that I was saying no to the business options. I would also turn down the offers to serve a different church. The River will be our life, I said. The smile on her face and the tears of joy we shared confirmed it. It was the launch of a new phase in our life together.

What I didn't know was that the elders who supported my former boss back when I was asked to resign had convened private meetings with two outside consultants.

It seems that the senior pastor who released both John Erwin and me had challenges of his own with the elders who, up until that point, had supported him. By the time our meeting for The River was held, this pastor also left the church he had served for seventeen years. I soon learned that *he* had plans to start a new church of his own.

With their senior pastoral leadership now all gone, the decision-making leadership that remained was deeply discouraged. Attendance declined precipitously. Income dwindled. These factors were not mere numerical statistics. These points of decline had more significant ramifications. The church had launched a capital campaign to build a worship center that would seat nearly three thousand people. The approvals were secured; capital had been raised. The lender made a firm commitment to the construction project. Additional adjacent property had been acquired. The design had been completed. The architects and draftsmen had put every detail for every room and every space on paper. The utilities were brought to the site. The concrete footings and foundation had been laid. The steel superstructure had been erected. The construction process was well under way and in competent hands.

The church appeared to be suffering an irreversible meltdown.

With the substantial decrease in attendance, the capital account set aside for the completion of the project dropped to dangerously low levels. The large building project was dependent on a vibrant congregation large enough to carry the cost. But midstream, that congregation was shell-shocked and demoralized. At one point, leadership actually commissioned a group of experts to assess the cost of taking the structure down. Canceling the entire project and clearing out the concrete and steel may be the only solution, they concluded.

If we had an enemy hell-bent on the destruction of this body of believers; if the intent was to extinguish the remaining light they shone in their community, it would be difficult to conjure up a more effective scenario than the one unfolding as the outside world watched. It broke my heart to see what was happening. There was nothing I could do. I have never felt more helpless. We were moving forward with our plans for The River with a collection of bright, vigorous staff and eager supporters that confirmed my sense that this vision should not be abandoned. But at the same time, I grieved over the turmoil at the church I unwillingly left behind.

And then . . . the telephone rang.

WHERE IS THIS GOING?

I was surprised by the sound of the voice on the other end. No small talk. He jumped right in.

"Matthew, the elders want to have a meeting with you," he said. His tone was friendly and affirming. "We have some things we need to say. It is very important to us."

His demeanor caused me to drop my defenses. This was the posture of reconciliation. And it took my breath away. "Of course," I said. What else could I say? "When and where?"

I hit the *END* button on my cell and sat down in the living room. I needed to think. Wow. Could this be happening? For months I harbored a bitterness I could not shake. I had been misunderstood. Branded. Discounted. Dismissed. They showed me the door. They relayed their opinion that day: I was guilty of poisoning the well. I had been the spoiler. They locked me out of my office, packed my stuff, and put the boxes on my front porch the day after I left.

Mardi walked in and saw me sitting with a blank stare aimed at the window. "What is it?" she asked.

As I explained the brief conversation on that call from that elder from the church we had served for so many years, the church that let me go, she walked over to me as she often does with an empathy that makes her the most significant person in my world, and she put her arms around me and simply whispered, "Wow." She nodded as she mulled over the news.

"That's big," she added.

> I looked around the room. No longer was I in the company of my accusers.

We laughed out loud, a nervous kind of laugh, and held each other tight. What does this mean? Where is *this* going? All of those questions fell in on us.

As I entered that familiar conference room, I tried to disguise my anxiety. I had been tentative about going back. The wood-paneled room and large table surrounded by high-backed leather chairs was the same. The last time I sat here with these leaders, they confirmed the verdict delivered by my superior that dizzying day after golf. They told me—right here at this same conference table, in no uncertain terms—why I had to go.

Meetings have personalities. The word *ambiance* applies. In our parlance, the "sense of the meeting" is essential. The last time I was here, the sense of the meeting was clear. They wanted me gone, and they had marshaled their best case. It was business. I tried not to let it be personal. But it was.

That was then. This time, the sense of the meeting was entirely different. I had a long history with these people. I could tell the moment I walked into the room. There was a palpable heaviness. I could see it in their eyes, hear it in their voices, even at the greeting. The ambiance was sober, serious. They shook my hand with respect. They all made eye contact. Several of them embraced me. They pointed me to my seat at the table.

There was a sincerity and an authenticity that stirred a powerful emotion that welled up inside me before a word was spoken. I looked around the room. No longer was I in the company of my accusers. These were my friends.

A bottle of water helps. I had mine with me. I took my place at the end of the conference table, took a sip from the bottle, looked around the table, and said something neutral like, "Well, here we are."

Muted laughter broke the spell.

"WE WERE WRONG"

The chairman spoke first. "Matthew, we have gathered today for one purpose. There is a single agenda item, and nothing else."

He had my attention. The others, I could see, were in complete agreement. They nodded in my direction.

He paused, took a long breath. "Matthew, we have come to realize that we were wrong about you. We made some serious mistakes. And we are paying a high price for those mistakes."

I was completely disarmed. What he said was consistent with what I sensed from the moment I walked in. But even so, these words pierced through whatever guard I had left. There is something about humility, something that happens in the presence of true remorse. It defuses your defenses. It extinguishes your need for retaliation. Whatever thoughts you might have about revenge evaporate.

He went on.

"We are here to admit our mistakes. We know that we have injured you. We didn't listen when we should have. We didn't hear what you were trying to say."

It almost seemed surreal to be hearing these words. I had assumed for months that I would just have to live with the judgments that were made back when we were all just trying to get along. Back when my world collapsed. Paul and Barnabas separated ways. Paul shook the dust off his feet. I knew I just had to move on, make the best of it. And now, here I was in the room with a group of sincere people who wanted nothing less than reconciliation. Maybe even forgiveness.

"We are sorry, Matthew," he continued. "*I* am sorry." Tears came to his eyes. He cleared his throat; took a sip from *his* water bottle. It validated the sincerity of his heartfelt words. "We are here to apologize for the wrong. We intend to make it right."

My guardedness and whatever resentments lingered inside me disappeared in those unexpected moments. In a way I had never known before, to my complete surprise, I began to come to terms with my own culpability in this thing. It was as though *their* spirit of contrition invited mine to come to the surface.

> To my complete surprise, I began to come to terms with my own culpability in this thing.

But the meeting was only beginning. Each guy around the table took a turn. They repeated the chair's sentiments in their own words, and added details from their own interaction with me through those days of crisis.

I had never experienced anything like this. It was like a scene taken directly from the Scriptures. Jesus often talked about mutual forgiveness. Paul made unity a distinct priority. David talked about how pleasant and good unity can be. And here it was unfolding before me on a level that was completely new, real. Like living water.

When it was over, it was a rare moment of dumbstruck. I didn't know what to say. Emotion got hold of me. I grabbed my water bottle.

"I'm sorry, too," I squeaked out.

Then the chairman spoke one last time. "All we want is another meeting, Matthew." I nodded in agreement and said, "OK."

"Let's make it next week," he said. I agreed, and we adjourned.

In the week that followed, I went back to my newly formed staff at The River. Plans were in full swing. We had a Christmas Eve event planned. The performing arts center was booked. We located a perfect facility to build our worship center and offices. We were in negotiation with the owner and contractors for the tenant improvements. We were in design mode.

Our website was operational. We had filled it with content. We stated our mission, purpose, and values. We identified a church-planting group and planned to associate with them. I was already involved in the lives of our people as a pastor. There were counseling calls, weddings in the works, and even a funeral.

We were committed to families. That meant gearing up a children's program that would be more than child care. We would design a welcoming entrance that would attract the kids. We wanted them to think of going to church as the best part of their week. We would staff it with people who knew how to make it active, informative, and fun. There would be bright colors, sound, staging, and lighting.

We would partner with other ministries that fill specific needs. There would be missions outreach. All of it was in place. Ready to go.

"They want you back," one of them said abruptly. He was referring to the elder meeting at the former church.

"Maybe," I said. "But it's not going to happen."

That meeting with those elders unsettled my new team. As powerful and as meaningful as it was to be moving toward reconciliation, I still could not see us coming together, even if those elders did want me back. "Let's get back to work," I said.

So our River team had plenty to do. Our October event had resulted in an explosion of enthusiasm. It was hard to wait until Christmas Eve for our next gathering. We planned to tap into all the glow and wonder of that celebration. We rented a large performing arts hall.

As we planned, I met again with the elders from my former church as I had promised I would. My River team was skeptical. Nothing was hidden. Some of our key supporters shared the concern.

Their position was clear: I had been banished from the church back in the spring. Whatever problem they had over there was not *my* problem.

Or The River's problem. It was *their* problem.

Nevertheless, I had promised to meet the elders, and we met. We convened again in that same conference room a week after the first meeting, as scheduled. There were many memories attached to that room, but none more vivid than the day I was sent away packing and then the day, six months later, just one week ago, of reconciliation. I understood that these good leaders had a serious problem. Because of the spirit in the room, which continued in this meeting, I felt I owed them a hearing.

My staff was right. This time, they made that not-so-modest proposal.

They told me they wanted me to pray about coming back to the church. They openly confessed that they misunderstood my role back before I left. They read the information John and I put forward on our website. They understood that our plans for The River were an extension of what I was trying to do back when I was on their staff as the executive pastor. They felt the passion. They resonated with the vision. They shared the goals and objectives. They affirmed together that what they read was consistent with what they believed should be foundational to the next phase of their church. They asked me to begin praying about returning and implementing the plans we had for The River right there in the church I'd left behind.

As I left that meeting, I don't know how to describe the way I felt other than to say I was stunned. The proposal, and the way it was presented to me, was completely unanticipated. Unexpected. I went home first, and sat down with Mardi and recounted the entire morning. As I promised I would, we prayed.

And then I shared it all with my River team.

In those first few meetings, I still could not get my arms around the idea of returning to the church. There were too many questions. My wife and my staff articulated them better than I. Why do you need to be the one to rescue them? What about the plans for The River? They rejected you once; what makes you think it won't happen again? Why take on that monumental challenge of the baggage of debt and staff and programming when we are well on our way to an unencumbered fresh start?

As the meetings progressed, the elders were more and more candid about the situation at the church. In one final meeting, they laid out the numbers. The situation was even worse than we feared. Far worse.

We went ahead with our plans for Christmas Eve at The River. The fellowship of families, husbands and wives, grandmas and grandpas, singles and young folks and children filled with anticipation and joy, well, we all glowed like the candles surrounding the room.

At the end of the evening, I invited those who wanted to be a part of the launch of the new church to stay behind for a brief update. As we gathered, everyone quieted down. I stood before them and said thank you. Many already had sacrificed time and energy and resources.

Then I told them candidly about my meetings with the leadership of my former church. I could see the look of puzzlement. I understood, I said. I don't know where this is leading, I told them, but Mardi and I were praying. I invited them to do the same.

As we concluded, I made as strong a statement as I could: the vision that gave birth to The River is alive and well.

TO THE COMMUNITY AND THE WORLD

Soon, it was a new year.

I had a decision to make, the most difficult of my life. I gathered together my most trusted counselors and advisors.

On the one hand, I had no interest in shifting our plans for The River. Over the months of dreaming and planning, my sense of call to pastoral ministry had been renewed, maybe even reborn. There were other fine churches. The invitations were there. Some attractive business opportunities opened up as well. But nothing seemed as right to me as The River. Our staff gelled. Leaders emerged. A facility became available. We began designing the tenant improvements.

I met once more with their elders. They told me they had carefully re-viewed and studied our business plan for The River. They believed it was exactly what their church needed. They believed the best possible venue for this vision was the 2,800-seat worship center under construction. They wanted me to be lead pastor and bring this new vision to the entire congregation.

I asked them to define "Lead Pastor." They told me I would have the authority to build the staff. I would set the vision. They understood that the changes required a review of the entire organization. We reviewed the numbers. We understood that the building project was behind schedule both financially and in the construction. The enormity of the shortfall emerged: the project required an additional fourteen million dollars to be completed.

Once again, we prayed. I talked to my council of advisors. I talked to my River staff.

I decided that I would have to be direct with the elders who invited me to return. If I were to come back, several conditions needed to be under-stood. First, my staff at The River would all come with me. The new elder board would be a blend of existing elders and River leadership. And most important, we all had to agree to one philosophical point: we would not be an inwardly focused church. All of our program design would be directed toward reaching out to our community and world. That was nonnegotiable.

On the financial side, I made clear that if we were to move forward, I would personally commit to finding half of what was needed to cut the deficit in current donations in my first ninety days as lead pastor. I ex-pected all of the leadership to join me in that effort and share that com-mitment. That would be seven million dollars.

It was a God-sized challenge. I knew it would be impossible in my own strength. It would require a new level of trust from us all.

We went back, as is our tradition, to the sense of the meeting.

The *sense* was unanimous. My River staff and leadership, the elders, and Mardi and I . . . all of us agreed we would move forward.

Nearly seven million dollars would need to materialize.

The meetings began.

Chapter 4

CONVERSION

THE STAGE FOR THE DECLARATION of Independence from casteism was set.

The massive crowd gathered, crammed into limited space. The sound system boomed across the open area and spilled into the crowded city streets of New Delhi. News crews were everywhere. Amateurs captured the spectacle on their pocket-sized digital cameras.

Ram Raj took to the microphone and issued an enthusiastic welcome. He identified himself as a Dalit, an untouchable. He announced the purpose of the meeting: to renounce Hinduism's hold on him and everyone who would make the same claim.

Today, he said, he would reject the religion of his birth and embrace Buddhism just as his hero and predecessor, B. R. Ambedkar, did in 1956. And together with all those assembled, he would declare the Dalit people free to choose; freedom to convert to any religion or no religion at all. The chains of untouchability would be broken. It would be a historic, watershed pronouncement.

Standing at the podium, he was overcome by the moment, a moment he had worked toward most all his adult life. It was his life mission.

"Today, I am no more an *achoot* (untouchable)." His voice cracked with emotion. "The Hindu gods and goddesses have only given Dalits indignity, hunger, and slavery. We refuse to accept this code of domination anymore. Dalits must liberate themselves from the shackles of their oppressed past and usher in a new renaissance through education and the awareness of human rights."

> Udit disassociated himself from his given Hindu name. He chose a new name. It signaled a new identity.

And with ceremonial dignity, after others addressed the crowd, he submitted himself to Bhante Buddhapriya Rahul, a Buddhist monk, who gave him the *diksha*, and according to tradition, shaved his head as the people cheered.

Next came the name-changing ceremony.

Up until this point in his life, Udit had been known as Ram Raj. "Ram" was his given Hindu name, after the seventh Avatar (incarnation) of Vishnu (the supreme deity). His parents gave him this name as an honor to one of their gods—a god who, because of their status as Dalits, they were not allowed to worship.

On this day of renunciation, Udit disassociated himself from his given Hindu name. He chose a new name. It signaled a new identity. And so, with a gleaming, clean-shaven head, the Buddhist monk Rahul stood with Ram at center stage and introduced the organizer of the event, for the first time, with a new name.

He called it out: "Udit Raj!"

And the massive crowd roared its approval. *Udit* is translated "risen."

"Udit Raj!" he shouted.

"*Udit Raj!*" the crowd repeated. "*Udit Raj!*" A chant began.

Udit Raj quieted the crowd and continued to speak. He spoke more fully on the Hindu caste system's hold on India's burgeoning population of over one billion people. He rehearsed the story of his hero and mentor, B. R. Ambedkar, who set the stage for the liberation of an entire people, the Dalits. He spoke of dignity and the power of education. He recited the Twenty-Two Vows written nearly fifty years before by Ambedkar, which include the following affirmations.[1]

✤ I shall have no faith in Brahma, Vishnu and Maheshwara, nor shall I worship them.

✤ I shall have no faith in Gauri, Ganapati, and other gods and goddesses of Hindus nor shall I worship them.

✤ I do not and shall not believe that Lord Buddha was the incarnation of Vishnu. I believe this to be sheer madness and false propaganda.

✤ I shall not allow any ceremonies to be performed by Brahmins.

✤ I shall believe in the equality of man.

✤ I shall endeavor to establish equality.

✤ I shall have compassion and loving-kindness for all living beings and protect them.

✤ I shall not steal.

✤ I shall not tell lies.

✤ I shall not commit carnal sins.

✤ I shall not take intoxicants like liquor or other drugs.

✤ I shall endeavor to follow the noble eightfold path and practice compassion and loving-kindness in everyday life.

✤ I renounce Hinduism, which is harmful for humanity and impedes the advancement and development of humanity.

Most everyone in the crowd repeated the vows after him.

And then Udit Raj made an unprecedented move. He turned to one side and spoke directly to a group of friends at the front. They were Christians. He thanked them warmly for their support and solidarity in courageously standing up for Dalit liberation.

He turned to the crowd and declared, "Dalits! Get out of casteism! All human beings are equal! Go on and convert to any faith of your choice!"

He turned to the high-rise office buildings in the distance.

"Let my people go!" he shouted. The crowd cheered its approval.

Raj continued, "If a Dalit chooses Christianity and decides to follow Jesus Christ, he is free to do so. It is a matter of conscience. A matter of choice. A matter of freedom of religion! A Dalit who converts as a Christian, under the established constitution of India, has the full rights of citizenship! There is no discrimination in the eyes of justice!"

The crowd roared again.

And after a few more pointed remarks, he introduced his friend and colleague in freedom's cause, Dr. Joseph D'souza.

OPENING THE GATES

D'souza had walked through this minefield with his friend, now Udit Raj. He understood the risks. He grasped the political dynamics. D'souza, as executive director of one of the largest evangelical Christian organizations in all of India, understood fully why this event did not give an open invitation to Dalits to declare themselves Christians and publicly convert. He and his staff had closely followed the unfolding of events that led to this landmark gathering. After all the years of struggle, he celebrated this open indictment of a Hinduism that held untold millions under a cruel yoke of oppression for several millennia. To him, this historic moment was a breakthrough of monumental proportion.

He also knew the risk of appearing on this stage. He solicited all his friends and associates for prayer. As he approached the microphone, with a bulletproof vest wrapped around his chest under a white shirt and black traditional Indian suit jacket, in the heat of the late-morning sun, he later told his supporters that he felt both a serenity and quiet confidence. He welcomed this unprecedented opportunity to address this massive crowd and all the media, cameras, and microphones, as a follower of Jesus.

Raj put his arm around D'souza, warmly greeting him for all to see. Then Raj turned to the microphone. "This is my friend Dr. Joseph D'souza. He is a Christian leader. I have asked him to speak to you today. Give him a hearty welcome!" and Raj started the applause.

"Thank you, Dr. Udit Raj," D'souza said. Polite applause. And then he turned back to the crowd with a tone of warmth and acceptance and affirmation.

"My precious brothers and sisters, you have been created in the image of God. From the beginning of time to this very day, God loves you. The church in India has in too many ways failed to live up to the demands of the Gospel. It is wrong for the church of Jesus Christ to be segregated by caste. It is a sin." He paused for a moment, just to let the power of that assertion set it. "We repent of this sin." Another pause.

"Today, we make a solemn vow to be obedient to Jesus Christ who came to break down the dividing walls and open the doors."

"I come to you today speaking in the name of Jesus Christ, proclaiming His love and His mercy for us all."

The crowd was not quite sure how to respond. There was more polite applause here and there, but D'souza's words were remarkable. These Dalits had never before heard such a confession from a Christian leader, much less an *upper-class* Christian leader.

"I come to you today speaking in the name of Jesus Christ, proclaiming His love and His mercy for us all. Jesus came to set the captives free. Whomever the Son sets free is free indeed. The gates are open wide. Please remember, we love you with the love of Jesus Christ unconditionally.

We love as He loved. Without reservation. Without condition. Now and forever."

D'souza and Raj embraced in a display of solidarity and friendship.

The crowd applauded again, this time with enthusiasm and appreciation. Later, people would say, you could feel freedom in the air. A heavy burden lifted. This was a new face for the Christian message. D'souza and one other Christian leader, Dr. K. P. Yohannan, who also addressed the crowd with a similar message, had broken down an impenetrable barrier that existed since the birth of the Christian church in India over fifteen hundred years ago.

The seeds for Global Freedom were planted.

When I compiled my research on Udit Raj and read the accounts of Joseph's appearance that day in November 2001, I was filled with emotion. The courage. The grace. The power of his declaration. It all moved me to tears.

I understood why I had been so affected by that first meeting with Dr. D'souza in Hyderabad on my first trip in 2007. At the time, I had no way of knowing the scope of his impact on the nation. But on that platform, six years earlier, with God's protective care surrounding him, a vision was born within D'souza for Dalit freedom. And that is the vision that was transferred to me.

Later, Dr. D'souza reflected on that astonishing day. He said, in a written communiqué to his supporters and friends:

"Tens of thousands of Dalits flowed to the Ambedkar Bhavan (in spite of all the official attempts to prevent them) to reject the caste system and the Hindu system that imposed this inhuman social and spiritual [bondage] on them for over three millennia. The amazing thing about the crowds was that so many women turned up for the conversion ceremony. . . .

"For those of us who were guests on that day, the conversion ceremony was a revelation. The symbolism of it was powerful. First a Dalit Indian

Buddhist monk shaved the head of [Udit] Raj and administered the oaths. Such religious rites can only be performed by Brahmins according to the caste system. Next a series of vows were read out and agreed to. Some of them were developed by Ambedkar. In the vows was the rejection of the gods that had failed the Dalits and the system that had oppressed them. . . .

"This mass conversion will have major impact on the nation socially, politically and spiritually. The main speech [by Udit Raj] had a few major themes—first, the rejection of Hinduism and the caste system. Second, the [unchecked, forceful] oppression of the Sangh Parivar and the BJP. Third, for the first time in many, many decades the Christian church was defended openly from a public platform in the glare of international media and the right of the Dalits to seek solidarity with Christians. . . .

"This was [all] against the backdrop of the VHP accusation that this event was a Christian conspiracy. There was huge applause to this solidarity between Christians and Dalits. . . .

"Many hundreds of Christian leaders from India and some from the West were present to witness the event and express solidarity with the Dalits as they sought liberation . . . We were there as invitees and guests to their function . . . We were there to support their freedom of conscience and choice in the face of severe opposition . . . We firmly believe that the Dalit–Christian solidarity declared in Hyderabad will continue solidly in the days ahead . . . That we were there because Jesus loved them and that we were committed day and night in the years ahead to bring to them the incredible love of Jesus both in action and in word. . . .

"The spontaneous applause and the warmth of the Dalits to the presentation told us that the church's courageous stand in standing with the Dalits at this time was indeed from God. And now the whole church was faced with the incredible challenge of doing what it said it would do because the Dalits want us to come among them. . . .

"The public nature of these pronouncements cannot be underestimated . . . Christians were wise during the event. Some provided food packets for people, but most of all there was interaction and brotherhood as human beings. Christian love was demonstrated in whatever way possible. We followed the directions given by the Dalit leaders since it was their event on which they had worked so hard. . . .

"Because each one there knew that they could end up being targets, Christian courage was in full display."

—Reflections of Dr. Joseph D'souza

November 5, 2001

Targets. And in the months and years that followed, they would be just that.

NOTES

1. From www.ambedkar.org, adapted.

Chapter 5

GLOBAL FREEDOM

VISION IS NOT A CURE-ALL.

I have known pastors who jump from one great vision to the next, leaving their folks in a muddled state of confusion. Expectations raised can become expectations unrealized, and the result is disappointment. Discouragement. Vision can come across as some sort of gimmick, a contrivance to build enthusiasm and momentum. Beware: smart people are discriminating when it comes to vision.

Be prepared, too. If a genuine vision is big and compelling and designed to expand the kingdom of God, then there will be opposition. Some of it will be subtle. Some will be frontal and direct. Some will be downright demoralizing. With no real vision to contend with, our enemy doesn't have a lot to do. But when a vision captures something of the heart of God, be ready. Opposition will come. Be sure of it.

I knew we needed a God-sized vision to capture the hearts and minds of our people. We had the capacity. We are blessed with an enormous talent pool. Our folks come from high-level positions representing nearly every profession. Our people understand the basic principle: "To whom much is given, much will be required." Many were ready to take on the challenge.

When I was in that low period of doubt and questioning just after I left the church, I never imagined that within a year, I would be back in the lead post. We faced a major crisis, but through it all, our leadership, both the elders and the staff, proved to be godly. A spirit of humility pervaded our place; everyone stepped up. Our people worked hard. They made considerable sacrifices. We believed together that God called us to impact our community. We were growing. Month after month, people came to faith in Christ. New initiatives emerged that had broad impact. Community leaders became a part of our church family. Students celebrated new life. Children were cared for and taught. Marriages were strengthening. A stream of new babies and their parents were dedicated.

> We would not be a comfortable suburban church, content to celebrate our success in the construction of a shiny new facility.

When we finally opened the newly constructed worship center, we stood united in our praise to an amazing God.

We had our share of misfires. There were seven consecutive announcements of our move-in date for the Worship Center. Seven times, there were last-minute delays and postponements. But finally the day came. Many of our people would consider the opening of our 2,800-seat auditorium to be an arrival. A destination reached. The seven million dollars came in—on time.

But on that day, as I had made clear, we were all eyewitnesses. The elders stepped up. All of us were tempered by the near-the-brink disaster. Donors contributed, large and small. Construction resumed.

And our staff stepped up, too.

We would not be a comfortable suburban church, content to celebrate our success in the construction of a shiny new facility. The dedication of the building would not be the arrival. Rather, it would be a launch pad for new beginnings. Our identity would inevitably change. Expectations would increase. New doors of opportunity would open. We were facing many unknowns.

But there was one thing that was for sure: we were committed to an outward focus. It was the beginning of a new journey, a new start.

JOSHUA PACKS HIS BAGS

So we planned a celebration. And in the planning, I identified in a whole new way with a character in the Bible: Joshua. He grew up in the company of one of God's choicest servants, Moses. The time arrived when the baton was passed.

Joshua came to the edge of the Jordan River. Without seeking the position, he found himself responsible. As he looked over the water flowing southward from the Sea of Galilee to the Dead Sea, he understood. There would be surprises. There would be disappointments. There would be opposition. There would be distractions.

I thought a lot about his preparation for that defining moment.

As a young boy in Egypt, he watched his parents labor under the cruel whips of Egyptian masters. He listened at night as he heard stories of the God of Abraham who was promised a land and a nation.

He was curious about the pharaoh's kingdom; his staggering wealth. From a distance, he saw the massive works of art adorning the great cities and the stunning palaces. Some speculate that he watched his own people work on the pyramids and the great stone face of the Sphinx. He listened to his relatives complain about working conditions, and some would even speak of freedom. But then word began to circulate among the Hebrews that one of their own had appeared in Pharaoh's court. "Let my people go!" he cried.

Moses inspired Joshua. Most were skeptical. Few had yet developed a confidence in God that would cause them to believe in the possibility of liberation from their slavery. It seemed hopeless. Joshua, a youngster, listened and watched with wide-eyed admiration as Moses' demand became more and more believable.

Then Joshua joined six hundred thousand of his fellow slaves and their families, and followed Moses in that great escape from their terrible bondage in Egypt.

Joshua witnessed God's provision in the desert wilderness. He took note of all Moses' moves. Joshua emerged as a strong warrior.

In a battle with the Amalekites, young Joshua took command. His mentor, Moses, went to the top of a hill and watched the battle progress. Joshua would look up to the crest of the mountain at his teacher and coach, Moses, who held his hands high. As long as Moses could be seen with his arms outstretched, the army of Israel prevailed. If he grew weary and dropped his arms for a rest, the Amalekites would surge ahead. It was as though Joshua needed the emotional and spiritual strength of his mentor leader. So Moses, weary, got some help from his brother Aaron and his friend Hur. They propped up his arms, holding them high, and Joshua won the battle.[1]

It would be a signal moment in Joshua's career.

When Moses ascended Sinai to meet with God and receive the Law, Joshua was chosen to accompany him. Joshua witnessed the entire event firsthand. And then Joshua stood with Moses after that life-changing forty-day encounter with God on the mountain. They returned with the stone tablets, only to find the people carousing in a raucous out-of-control party around a handmade, false god. Joshua shared Moses' despair, frustration, and rage. The two of them bonded as a father and son would.

Joshua watched his people suffer, confined by the cruel chains of slavery. He was there when one of his own emerged as a champion of liberation. It was no wonder that Joshua, a bright, curious energetic boy, followed Moses' every word. He became Moses' aide. He proved himself on the battlefield. He watched Moses deal with crisis after crisis, all the while keeping faith.

After forty years of hardship and victory, the traveling band of the children of Abraham reached the eastern banks of the Jordan River. Moses handpicked twelve brave and fit warriors to launch a clandestine operation. They would secretly cross the river and make a general study of the land. They would locate cities and strongholds. They would scope out fertile, wet pastureland. They would collect samples of crops. They would identify water sources, map out the terrain. They would study demographics, determine population centers, and assess the capacity of the people for war. How fierce would be their defense? Moses wanted a complete report.

So the people prayed for them. These were the best of the best, the pride of each tribe. Joshua was one of them. The people waited nervously for the results of the contingent's report. They knew what was at stake. This would be a test.

The twelve scouts returned to the camp on the eastern side of the Jordan. The people gathered eagerly to hear the news. Together, the spies confirmed the richness of the land before them. It was abounding in resources. They found water sources that filled the cisterns and flooded the fields. There was grain for bread. Fruit in abundance. They put their samples on display. Then their tone changed. There were also fortified cities. On the other side, veteran warriors were ready in waiting, capable of a fierce defense. The fighting men were strong and tall and ferocious.

"Giants!" they proclaimed with fear in their voices, looking to one another for affirmation. The majority nodded with conviction. They reported their summary conclusion: a full ten of the twelve recommended scrubbing the foolhardy line of attack. Forget it, they said straight-out. No way. We must abandon this ridiculous plan. It is mass suicide.

The people listened in rapt silence. Many of them felt relief. "Yes!" they shouted. "Let's give up on this insane idea before we are all killed."

But two of them disagreed with the other ten. Only two. Caleb spoke first. He held up his hands, signaling silence. "We should go up and take possession of the land, for we can certainly do it."[2]

That assertion stopped the discussion cold. Is he *serious?* The other ten spoke up. Their voices screeched incredulity. Their description of the foe intensified. They called on every hyperbole in their native tongue. "We will surely die!" they shouted. They turned on the messengers.

Then Joshua spoke. "The land we passed through and explored is exceedingly good. If the Lord is pleased with us, he will lead us into that land, a land flowing with milk and honey, and will give it to us."[3]

That is when serious, angry opposition gathered momentum. Some conspired to have the two dreamers stoned to death.

But the courageous pair, these two sons of Abraham, prevailed: Caleb and Joshua.

In a sweet passage, as Moses reaches the end of his long and event-filled life, he chooses Joshua to assume his charge. The promises will be passed to him. He will be blessed. He will be victorious.

And in the transition, several key phrases are repeated over and over again. Be strong. Be courageous. Do not be afraid. The Lord your God is with you, wherever you go.

Joshua is one of my heroes. I identify with him. I have seen people who live in bondage, longing for escape. I have seen God call men and women to lead them out of that bondage into a glorious freedom. I have seen it in our church. The Dalit people are like the children of Israel. Many have been set free. They have become models for me.

I have had a Moses in my life, a man who opened doors for me. One who believed in me. One who celebrated my successes and helped me get back up when I fell down. When I was in the heat of the battle, I looked over my shoulder to see if I still had his blessing, and up there on the hill, he watched, with his hand raised in approval.

Come to think of it, over the years I have had more than one Moses: a veritable team of mentors who have believed in me and helped me.

Despite this unconditional support of those who have gone before me, like Joshua, I also have heard all the complaints. When it seemed that most everyone missed the vision of God's blessing to come, I have been there. I have heard people bring their gripes, their grievances, their fears, their doubts, their "common sense," and I have observed as they rally others into a strategy of retreat and withdrawal. I have listened in as initiatives for kingdom ministry have been abandoned and needy people ignored. I have heard about the "giants" and the probable calamity. I have seen believers give up before they have even tried. Every time I have witnessed these things, I have wanted to shout in a protest of my own, like Joshua and Caleb, and counter the argument. Sometimes I have stood against those who want to give up, but not often enough. None of this makes me better than anyone else. Joshua and Caleb are my heroes: their inextinguishable confidence in the power of God to do the impossible inspires me.

For reasons I never fully understood, like Joshua, I was asked to lead. Just as Moses and the people blessed Joshua, I felt called and blessed by the elders and the people of our church. I had so many questions. There were so many unknowns. The task seemed overwhelming and in so many ways unattainable.

God came to Joshua and simply said, "Pack your bags." Get the people ready. We are about to move out. We are going to cross that river and head out on the other side to the place that I have promised. I told you it would be good, that there would be milk and honey there. But it will not come easily. There will be a cost, but there will also be rest and blessings that you cannot even imagine.

The Lord added, "Just remember this:

Be strong and courageous.

Do not be afraid.

Do not be discouraged.

I will be with you wherever you go."[4]

Joshua knew where he was going. West. Over the river. He had his orders: conquer the land.

TIME TO MOVE ON . . . BUT WHERE?

We, too, had our orders. So we launched the new phase of ministry with weekend celebration services that broke all attendance records. There was a spirit of joy and anticipation I will never forget. Our worship team blew out the windows with praise and thanksgiving that drew us all together. I preached a sermon on Joshua.

The stage was set. We were prepared to launch new initiatives. We knew that we needed time for healing. We wanted more than anything else to be a healthy church, ready to take on the challenges of this new road ahead.

Our beautiful new facility was not the Promised Land. It was the Jordan River.

I did understand this: our beautiful new facility was not the Promised Land. It was the Jordan River.

When that throng followed Moses for forty years through the desert wilderness and finally arrived at the Jordan River, many argued, "Let's drop our roots right here on the banks of the waterway. It's a perfect place for our crops and livestock." But Moses knew, and Joshua knew, that this was just the starting point.

Some considered the completion of the building our destination, our destiny. When we filed into the new arena-sized room and found our own comfortable theater seat, the temperature was perfectly controlled. The lighting carefully gauged to suit the mood of the occasion and the preset plans on the stage. The sound system was in perfect pitch with acoustical balance at every seat in the house. Some, I am certain, thought, "Finally. We have arrived."

So I gathered every bit of persuasive power I could pull together. I pored over my message all week. And on that weekend, I did the best I could to challenge our people to see this watershed day not as a crossing of the finish line but as a gathering at the starting line. I had our creative arts team play the soundtrack from the rock band Switchfoot:

"Welcome to the planet, Welcome to existence . . . I dare you to move."[5]

Generally, I am not big on issuing a dare, especially in a sermon. But Switchfoot's lyrics said it for me. We had seen amazing miracles. Many of our people had been set free—from the bonds of addiction, relational meltdowns, out-of-focus careers, the cruel weight of past mistakes, financial pressures, debt, disappointments, and calamity. The pain of loss. The penalty of bad choices. The consequence of disobedience. People set free of all that and more by the power of the Gospel. And now, God was showing us the blessing of community. The amazing visible, tangible result of generous giving. The glory of worship. The multicolored flight of open praise. The transforming power of the written Word read and taught and proclaimed. All of it made for an incredible weekend of celebration. It was not a time to stay put, content to observe. The Gospel of Jesus Christ dares us to move.

Like Joshua on the banks of the River Jordan.

Moses was buried under the soil of the desert way up there somewhere on the mountaintop, his leadership forever valued, but now set aside. Joshua turned west, filled up with the power of his commitment, the courage of the promise, the strength of his conviction, and dared those people to move. With God's help.

On the day of our new beginning, on the day when I started this new chapter in my leadership life, I had not yet seen Hyderabad. I did not know Dr. D'souza. I had not seen a Dalit slum or a Dalit school. I didn't know what was on the other side.

But we moved out. Ready. Open. Poised to act.

And just as He promised, God went with us.

The torch had been passed to us. We knew it that opening weekend. But the accomplishment of finally completing this magnificent facility did not bring us to a place of self-satisfied inertia. We all felt it that day. We were ready to take the dare and move out.

But where?

Sixteen months later, I woke up at three o'clock in the morning at the

Corporate Stay Hotel in Bangalore, India, captured by a vision to build schools for Dalit children. God got hold of me—and would not let me go.

WE ARE ALL DALITS NOW

A few days later, in New Delhi, I relaxed in a picturesque swimming pool with a friend and colleague in a hotel that was a considerable upgrade from the Corporate Stay. Brent Martz (our worship and arts team leader) and I reflected on our experience as we floated in the cool, crystal-clear waters. Both of us were ambivalent about the extravagance of swimming in this pool. It was a welcome taste of Orange County, California, on the other side of the globe. It seemed light-years away from the slums of Mumbai and Hyderabad and Bangalore and Kolkata and the rural expanse that covers a nation one-third the landmass of the United States and yet has over three times the population. But there we were in this opulent pool, surrounded by manicured gardens, carefully trimmed statuary, and bubbling fountains. And the slums, home to some 250 million Dalits, remained just down the street from our luxurious accommodations.

We came to the end of an exhausting journey. We had experienced information and sensory overload. We shared the conviction that God had met us here in India. We believed we found what we were looking for—a compelling vision, a God-sized goal. These were the kind of people Jesus targeted with love and mercy and compassion. We were tired, but exhilarated over the possibilities. We saw firsthand the evils of a system that rendered over a quarter of an entire population "untouchable." We saw it in the eyes of the children and the faces of the elderly. We understood that the illusion of a prosperous India only represented a small minority of the population. Because we were Americans, we not only could afford to stay in this beautiful hotel, but it made us feel as though we were at home. We were brought face-to-face with our own distorted sense of entitlement, our inflated expectations. The contradiction hurt. We had a love/hate relationship with a swimming pool. It made us laugh and cry at the same time.

It all triggered a long and deep conversation between the two of us, right there in those waters. We have been close friends since we were collegians. We agreed: we had found something we could give our lives to. It contained all the elements of the highest and best of God's work in the world. *Free the Dalits!* It became a battle cry for the two of us.

The Gospel of Jesus Christ became the power of God in ways we had not seen before. It is the power of God unto salvation—and a complete contrast to the message these people had heard all their lives. They were like the children of Abraham in bondage under the Pharaoh's cruel whips. We began to think of Dr. D'souza as a modern-day Moses. "Let my people go!" It was in his blood. We could see it in his eyes. We felt it in his heart.

Somehow, Jesus' prediction became a reality for us. He said that if we would take the time to help the helpless, He would meet us there. The scope and magnitude of the issues we talked about seemed so completely out of reach. In many ways, it was utterly simple. In other ways, it was downright complicated, overwhelming. We were caught in the tension between the possible and the impossible.

> We were caught in the tension between the possible and the impossible.

Building schools for children was possible. Eliminating the caste system in India seemed impossible. But we knew instinctively that the first would ultimately lead to the second. We developed a deep passion to bring young Dalit children the message that they are made in the image of God; that they have equal standing before their Creator among all humankind; to help them understand that there are no barriers, there are no limits; to teach them the redemptive power of the Gospel; to point them toward opportunity; to learn the language of empowerment and upward mobility in India: English. Feed them with good nutrition. Provide health care. Teach hygiene and preventive medicine. Surround them with love and affirmation and discipline and hope. We saw the transformation with our own eyes. And somehow we knew that if there were enough schools, enough children awakened to a new worldview that eventually the caste system itself would crumble under the terrible weight of its own cruel abuse. It would be exposed for what it really is: modern-day slavery.

The excitement of the thought made us both shiver in those cool, chlorinated waters. And that is when we made a vital connection: we understood that the plight of the Dalits is the plight of every person. Don't confuse what I'm saying here. The plight of the Dalits is uniquely dreadful. The hunger, the disease, the abuse, the exploitation, the violence against the body and spirit, the assault on human dignity, all of it palpable. Incomparable.

But there is a universal message here that extends beyond India's dark secret. It is the Dalit story, but it is also the human story. We are all vulnerable: the message of inadequacy, the burden of guilt, powerful barriers erected as boundaries within which we are confined. There is pressure to conform to the way things are, to accept the unacceptable without a thought toward breaking free. We can be caught in the structures of religion, culture, and ethnicity. They bind us to an aimless, purposeless existence. There appears to be no avenue of escape. We long to be free.

Brent and I went back and forth chatting there in the swimming pool, realizing that we were tapping into something huge. We pictured the streets of American cities where too many wander aimlessly, homeless. We thought about the African victims of AIDS caught in a cycle of tyranny and poverty for generation after generation of violence and heartache. And we talked about our upscale town and the lonely, self-medicated people behind those wrought-iron gates with manicured lawns and glittering fountains, harried and stressed in a mad search for just one more success. Imprisoned behind a guarded entrance.

There we were, two healthy young Americans lounging in a posh hotel in uptown New Delhi, surrounded by people working furiously to make us comfortable. But it was clear: we looked around at the other guests and knew immediately that wealth did not deliver on its promise. We could see emptiness and high-stress aimlessness here, too.

There is a longing in the human heart for freedom. It is a universal longing—and it is elusive. Some think that democracy will be enough, that a constitutional guarantee of freedom is sufficient. Others believe that the absence of restrictive rules and release from the pressure to conform to some long-standing, socially enforced tradition will bring freedom. The defeat of a despised enemy or carefully crafted legislation will deliver freedom, others say. All of these may open the door, but true freedom is something much more profound. Authentic liberation happens on the level of the human heart. Brent and I knew we were really talking about the liberating power of the Gospel of Jesus Christ. God's eternal plan for a lost world caught up in mortal conflict delivers a freedom that transcends every barrier, every boundary, every prison house, both real and imagined.

> The longing in the human heart for freedom is a universal longing —and it is elusive.

The pace of our dialogue quickened as our enthusiasm welled up. We moved from the pool to the lounge chairs to soak up some of the warm Indian sunshine. I do not remember which of us said it first. It could have been Brent. It could have been me.

"*Global freedom*—that's what we're talking about."

"Global freedom!" The phrase was spoken out loud for the first time.

That's it. Global Freedom.

We liked the sound of it. But even more, the potent meaning of the phrase gripped us. We were committed to the Dalit people of India—250 million of them, bound by a system that for more than three millennia condemned an entire population to a life of cruel abandonment, exploitation, isolation, oppression, and hardship—in summary, exclusion from all the benefits of the social order.

Global Freedom comes with a message of hope and transformation and liberation for all people. It is not the promise of a constitution or a legislative body. It is the work of God.

When a Dalit makes this declaration of independence, he or she is renewed in mind, body, and spirit. It is a complete and total paradigm shift. It is no magical formula, but it is a new beginning. Doors that were slammed shut generations ago are unlocked and opened wide. An eternal destiny has been redefined, redirected.

> When a Dalit finds the liberating power of the Gospel and begins a journey toward wholeness, he or she is setting the pace for the rest of us all over the world.

What we understood in that weighty conversation in the pool went beyond India and trailed all the way back home. When a Dalit finds the liberating power of the Gospel and begins a journey toward wholeness and meaning, he or she is setting the pace for the rest of us all over the world. The lower castes across India are longing for the same release. Africans, Chinese, Pakistanis, Koreans, Europeans, Latinos, Asians, and Americans—our neighbors in North Orange County, California—all of us. Everyone is on the hunt for this same freedom.

Global Freedom.

When we launched that summer Sunday back home in our new worship center, after seven failed attempts, we were determined to resist the temptation to view that big, beautiful space as a landing site.

I drew on the strength and courage that Joshua found there on the eastern bank of the Jordan River. I reminded our people of Moses' clarion call; his demand stated forcefully in the opulent courts of the Egyptian pharaoh: "Let my people go!"

But on that Sunday, I did not know any more than Joshua did where the journey might lead. I only knew that God had been faithful in bringing us to this amazing place in our personal and corporate history. I knew we could trust Him. This was not my story. It was God's story.

And remember, back on that watershed Sunday when we dedicated our new worship center, I had not yet set foot in Hyderabad or Bangalore or Pipe Village or a Good Shepherd School or the Corporate Stay Hotel. I had not yet shook the hand or made eye contact with the good Dr. D'souza or understood the journey that put him in a bulletproof vest on the platform of that pivotal, decisive event at the fairgrounds in New Delhi alongside Dr. Udit Raj in November 2001. I had not walked the makeshift streets of a Dalit slum, or considered the curious evils of untouchability. I had not met Dalits who had been transformed by the Gospel message. Nor had I heard the uniformed young students laughing or learning or singing in those unlikely classrooms.

I had not uttered the phrase "Global Freedom."

I only knew that God had the same message for me that He had for Joshua.

Be strong and courageous.

Do not be afraid.

I will be with you, wherever you go.

NOTES

1. See Exodus 17:10–13.
2. Numbers 13:30.
3. Numbers 14: 7–8.
4. Joshua 1:9, partly paraphrased.
5. Switchfoot, "Dare You to Move" from the album *Learning to Breathe* © 2007 Sony BMG Music Entertainment.

Chapter 6

RESISTANCE

Late 1990s–Bangalore and Orissa, India

MY INVESTIGATION into the Dalit freedom movement took me to some surprising, disturbing places.

I learned all I could about the November 2001 event that catalyzed the modern-day campaign: this is a battle against an evil form of social and political slavery. In this dark world, Christians have been and continue to be targets.

It is a documented fact.

I had to dig deeper, peel back some of the layers, and get myself into more of India's history to grasp the powerful dynamics of what we are facing today. I wanted to understand the context of the tensions that led to violence. Beneath the pleasing colors and the pleasant faces, those who press for change are at risk.

INDIA'S COMPLEX TAPESTRY

India has always been known as a land of romance, mystery, and exotic riches. It is a global economic and cultural force. The sheer size of the nation would be enough. Geographically, the twenty-eight states form the seventh largest nation in the world, well over a million square miles. Its people count is the second highest on earth: over 1.1 billion (just behind China's 1.3 billion). Its constitution is democratic; indeed, India is the most populous democracy in the world.

In its four-thousand-year history, India gave birth to four of the major world religions: Hinduism, Buddhism, Jainism, and Sikhism. Christianity arrived as early as the second century (some believe the first[1]), and along with Judaism and Islam, have existed for well over a thousand years in pockets all across the continent.

From the beginning of recorded history, India has been a player on the global stage. Rich in resources, exotic products and spices, and colorful silks and fabrics, India's trade routes made it the economic center of Asia. Alexander the Great conquered the known world. India was the one military victory he lusted after but would not win. It was beyond even his reach. When Christopher Columbus convinced Queen Isabella of Spain to bankroll his journey around the globe, it was the prospect of connecting with India that captured her imagination.

Columbus got his funding.

Throughout the last century, India was twice impacted by world war, and each time, its resources considered a major prize. But Britain controlled much of the commerce in the subcontinent.

Since just before the American Civil War, in 1856, the East India Company claimed control of the entire country. When India rebelled, the British monarchy sent its troops to quell attempts at independence. As Great Britain colonized India, the influence of the Empire took hold. Britain's influence could be seen in architecture, language, the court system, even the parliamentary procedure adopted by the government. But Indian culture remained intact. Hindi was the national business language and Hinduism the primary religion; to this day, more than 80 percent of the population of India is Hindu.

India struggled for independence for one hundred years. Under the dynamic, quiet leadership of Mahatma Gandhi, India won its freedom from British rule in 1947. A democratic constitution governed the new nation, a document largely drafted by Udit Raj's hero, B. R. Ambedkar. But by this time, India's institutions were steeped in British tradition. English trumped Hindi as the most profitable international business language. Upward mobility belonged to those who would play by Western rules. India was poised to embrace the new global economy, on a global scale.

Thomas Friedman, the *New York Times* foreign affairs columnist turned author, made his first visit to India in 2004. As a

> Upward mobility belonged to those who would play by Western rules.

student of the global economy, he had made serious statistical projections about the loss of commerce in the United States because of a phenomenon popularly dubbed "outsourcing." Outsourcing went beyond manufacturing. Jobs disappeared in the United States, the United Kingdom, and Europe, and proliferated in otherwise obscure corners of the globe.

So when the international expert from the world's largest newspaper went to India in 2004, as he explains in his groundbreaking book *The World Is Flat*, Friedman was shocked at what he found. To him, the notion that there would be a depletion of available jobs in the United States had been a distant projection. What he found in 2004 was instead a present reality. Outsourcing had already outpaced his prognostications. India's Silicon Valley (in Bangalore) had surpassed his wildest imaginations. The global economy is not coming, he declared. It is here.

The sleeping giant is awake. India has tapped into the global economy with vigor, intelligence, and determination. The possibilities for young, educated, ambitious Indians have never been greater. One out of every four Indians is under the age of twenty-five.

The call centers are only the tip of the economic iceberg. There is an explosion of innovation and manufacturing all up and down the streets of Mumbai, Bangalore, and Delhi. But go on outside, down the street, around the corner, and just next to the air-conditioned high-rise, you'll find the slums. Makeshift tents, no running water, overcrowded, with malnourished, illiterate untouchables of all ages. First you will meet the children. And then the elderly.

And you will know. This global power has a serious social problem.

BOLLYWOOD'S GIFT

When movie director Danny Boyle set out to produce a film based on a 2005 novel titled *Q & A* by Indian author Vikas Swarup, he did not imagine that the whole world would take notice. But it did.

To call *Slumdog Millionaire* a blockbuster hit would be an understatement. It won the Academy Award as best picture of the year in 2009—plus seven other Oscars.

> *Go outside, down the street, around the corner, and just next to the air-conditioned high-rise, you'll find the slums.*

Joseph D'souza considers the film a gift. Never in his wildest dreams did he imagine that there would be a partnership between Hollywood and Bollywood that would so clearly portray the plight of the Dalits of India with such force. In one year, 2009, the cause became an international topic of conversation.

In India, the film got a lukewarm reception: the portrayal of slum life; widespread; desperate poverty; child abuse; human trafficking; the underworld of the sex trade; the murder and pillaging by Hindu fundamentalists; and corruption in government and law enforcement. All the controversial messages based in reality contradict India's efforts to present itself to the world as a progressive, modern economic power. The country portrayed in the film is an India that officials prefer to sweep under a beautiful Indian-woven rug.

There are two Indias, it is often said. *Slumdog Millionaire* portrays them both in compelling, vibrant detail.

From my all-too-comfortable world in Southern California, I knew India was growing in influence. But I did not know the magnitude of the impact of the nation's role in the global economy. When we started, there was no Oscar-winning motion picture. The more I probed, the more I learned. We were not the only ones who noticed the disparity between the progress of upscale India and the plight of the untouchables. Even those who focused on the tech world could not avoid it.

We were onto something big. Really big.

When Thomas Friedman took his book *The World Is Flat* to television, he went to Bangalore for the Discovery Channel to speak to the beneficiaries of "outsourcing." Friedman's groundbreaking book makes the indisputable point that connectivity is bringing economic possibilities to the most remote corners of the globe. Old barriers like language, culture, national boundaries, governmental restrictions, and taxes, are becoming less and less a barrier to participation in the global economy. Where success was once out of reach, there is a new wave of access that supposedly "levels the playing field," making the world, well, "flat."

There is a new generation of Indian young people, ready and eager to land high-paying jobs in India's burgeoning technology sector. In his documentary for the Discovery Channel, Friedman tours some of the midnight call centers to interview both employers and workers. He follows them to school and speaks with their teachers and professors. He measures how these jobs change their life. He shows that these workers still make up a small percentage of the whole. Many are left out. Just outside the high-tech office building, the slums remain unchanged. The camera follows him out the door and around the corner. A slum neighborhood comes into view, right there in the shadow of the office complex.

"These are the Dalits of India," he says.

This is the other India. He speaks with a group of intellectuals who believe that globalization is destroying Indian culture. But, Friedman objects, what about the poor? Who is caring for them?

In the final segment of his documentary, interestingly, he visits a school for Dalit children. He speaks to the philanthropist who funded the construction and operation of the school with the fortune he earned in America, and from the computer center where the children learn, he says, "Our intent is for these children to break all the social barriers. We expect them to become the business, social, and intellectual leaders of the next generation."

Listen to the conversation Friedman has with the principal of this school just down the highway from Bangalore:

Friedman: "These students live in the neighborhood of the school. What do their parents do?"

School principal: "They belong to the lowest caste in society. They cannot associate with people of the upper castes because they will contaminate the air that they breathe."

Friedman: "They are 'untouchables.'"

School principal: "Yes, they are 'untouchables.'"

Friedman: "What are the conditions of the children before they come to your school?"

School principal: "Well, they are hungry. They are malnourished. They don't know what it is to have running water. They have to learn what it is to use a bathroom."

Friedman: "An hour from Bangalore, these high-tech cities we've been looking at, and they have never used a toilet."

School principal: "Less than an hour."[2]

India is a global power. The world is taking notice. But there is a dark reality just around the corner. A wildly popular motion picture gave the world a glimpse. Over 250 million souls, one quarter of India's population, live in suffocating, isolating, irreversible poverty.

It struck me. This three-time Pulitzer Prize–winning *New York Times* bestselling author saw what I saw. He was touched by it. He came to a similar conclusion. And in this final scene, he makes a striking, convincing argument: education is the single best hope for these children. So says Thomas Friedman. So we believe.

FACING TERROR

I wanted to know more about Gandhi's contemporary, Dr. Ambedkar, the man some call India's Thomas Jefferson. His story inspired Udit Raj. There had been resistance in Ambedkar's day. Resistance would be reawakened.

As Dr. Ambedkar learned back when India won its independence from Great Britain, a democratic constitution is no guarantee of liberty. While Article 25 of India's constitution (penned by Ambedkar) and the United Nations Declaration of Human Rights both declare freedom of religion for all India's citizens, several states still have anticonversion laws, as we have already noted. The cultural barriers remain firmly in place.

The religious establishment is predominantly Hindu. The culture of caste lives on. It has been woven into the fabric of Indian life since the beginning. For thousands of years, to move away from the caste of one's birth has been an unacceptable violation of Hindu tradition.

In the aftermath of the November 4, 2001, gathering in New Delhi, led by Dr. Udit Raj, a surge of self-determination swept Dalits all over India. But so did a wave of savage persecution, both against Dalits directly and against those who were believed to encourage liberation.

Dr. D'souza and his team knew it would come.

Raj and D'souza discussed the future of mass conversions. They knew the risks. But they also received urgent requests from cities and townships and villages all across the nation. In 2002, Raj spoke to *Christianity Today*. "We are going to make conversions a national phenomenon," Raj said. "I have a lot of appreciation for the Christians. They changed the lives of Dalits. Christians were the first to open [an] education system for Dalits, giving us a chance to be free and grow. People are converting to Christianity. Dalits have the right to choose any religion they want."[3]

Shortly after the major event in Delhi, reports of conversions all over

India began to surface. When D'souza agreed to appear with Udit Raj that day, he knew the risks. None were surprised by the aggressive efforts to stop the event. This kind of persecution was nothing new to the two leaders.

When they met the month before in Hyderabad and then in Bangalore to plan the November event, they and their support teams prayed fervently for protection. They understood the history of nationalist organizations.[4]

Death threats and intimidation intensified. A wave of innuendo and personal attacks hit the Internet and even the local press. For a North American to understand the nature of some of these groups, particularly the more radical among them, you might think of the Ku Klux Klan during the darkest days of the civil rights movement or radical Islamist terrorists such as Al Qaeda, plotting and executing terrorist strikes all over the world.

Non-Hindus, including Christians, have long been victimized by such terror in India. Freedom's cause proceeds at great risk.

GRAHAM STAINES AND THE "UNTOUCHABLE UNTOUCHABLES"

As a boy, Graham Staines loved the seacoast just about fifteen kilometers from his home in Palmwoods, Queensland, Australia, about a half-hour north of Brisbane. He was raised in a Christian home and had a curiosity about life beyond the vast seas. He also learned from his godly parents that Christians had a duty to care for the poor and needy. Later he would learn the term "disenfranchised."

As a young man, he learned about a leprosy settlement in the exotic land of India through a missionary connection in his little country church. In 1965, barely twenty years old, he made his way to Baripada in the northernmost part of the state of Orissa. He knew about the caste system's concept of untouchability. But, he surmised, those poor souls suffering from leprosy were a tragic redundancy—untouchable untouchables.

Graham studied the mythology of leprosy and overcame his natural aversion by reaching out, as Jesus did, to those who were despised and rejected. He found his life's calling. He associated with the Australian NGO (Non-Government Organization) registered in India as the Evangelical Missionary Society of Mayurbhanj. They had a long history of work with leprosy patients all over India.

In 1981, Graham met an attractive young woman visiting the settlement. They had an instant rapport; Gladys also felt an enormous affection for these forgotten people. When she sensed Graham's heart for their care, she was immediately drawn to his kindness and grace. The secluded leprosy patients clearly felt comfortable in his company.

They married two years later, after Gladys agreed to live in one of the poorest sections of Orissa. Not long afterward, their daughter and two boys arrived right there in an Indian hospital: Esther, Timothy, and Philip.

They would tell you that their commitment to God brought them both to India. Graham loved language and conversation. He became fluent in three local dialects: Oriya, Santhali, and Ho. He worked on several translations of the Bible. He taught Bible studies. He founded both the Mayurbhanj Leprosy Home and the Rajabasa Leprosy Rehabilitation Farm.

At the same time, Ravinder Kumar Pal, a Dalit himself, pursued his own education. How far he got in his university career is not clear. But he became convinced that Hinduism was under siege. He determined to do something about it. Initially, he taught school. But his campaign to stop the contamination of his country by intrusive forces from the outside became his full-time occupation.

He associated with a Hindu nationalist organization called the Bajrang Dal, the youth wing of the radical Vishwa Hindu Parishad. As a sign of his devotion, he changed his name to Dara Singh (after Dara Singh Randhawa, the famous Indian wrestler turned Bollywood actor).

As time passed, Dara Singh became more and more radical. He believed that secularists, Muslim and Christian groups from the outside, violated the anticonversion laws as they worked with Orissa's tribal people (aka: the untouchables). He accused them of bribery and corruption. He cited a clear example: cows were transported over state lines where they were butchered for their beef, and then the meat would be shipped back to his state for sale, profit, and illegal consumption, which, for Singh, was the destruction of a sacred animal and prohibited by the Indian constitution (Article 48).

Singh, his associates, and followers claimed that the "perpetrators" of crimes against the Hindu religion must be punished. They had no confidence that the courts would administer justice. So they made their own plan. "Justice" would be meted out—on their terms.

Back in Baripada, Orissa, a small conference was held in a remote forest next to a church in Manoharpur village of Orissa's Keonjhar district. It was an association of Christian workers who met to talk about the intricacies and nuances of evangelism. They also spoke of water projects and preventive medicine and hygiene. They prayed for one another. Studied their Bibles.

> The boys looked back at their father in horror. Graham knew immediately.

Worshiped. Encouraged each other. Graham brought his two young sons along with him, Timothy and Philip. After a long day of travel, and meetings that went past dark, they settled into their well-worn Willys jeep for a night's rest.

They drifted off to sleep.

Bang! Bang! A loud noise awakened them, just after midnight. Then, screaming and chanting of men's voices followed. It frightened the boys, still half asleep. Graham raised his head to look out the window, then over at his young sons.

Bright lights were trained on them from all sides. The boys looked back at their father in horror. Graham knew immediately.

This was a visitation of terror.

The gang of over a dozen men, faces covered, smacked the truck with bats, clubs, and batons. A headlight shattered. Graham and the boys tried to escape, but the doors of the jeep were jammed shut. Their panicked struggle proved futile. Several attackers surrounded the vehicle by the dim lamps and flashlights carried by their comrades. They were screeching, hooting, howling. The men outside lifted heavy canisters with open nozzles, pouring their contents on the vehicle with the three innocents trapped inside. With a gleam in their widened eyes, they danced in a trance-like frenzy. They doused the old oxidized truck, emptying the fuel cans on the hood, roof, windshield, bumpers and thick rubber tires. One of them ceremoniously tossed a lit match on the gasoline. A thunderous roar filled the night air and a bright light illumined the trees and the church and the faces of the mob.

Graham pulled his sons close with both arms and held them tight.

That was January 22, 1999.

Four years later, September 23, 2003, the *New York Times* published the following report:

> A court in Bhubaneshwar, the capital of Orissa State, today sentenced to death by hanging the ringleader of a Hindu mob that burned and killed an Australian missionary and his two sons.
>
> The ringleader, Dara Singh, and his 12 accomplices, who were sentenced to life in prison, were convicted last week of attacking the missionary, Graham Staines, and his sons Philip, 10, and Timothy, 6, as they slept in their jeep in an isolated village and then setting the vehicle afire.[5]

While Dara Singh confessed his guilt before an open court, he now denies that he was there. Some believe Mr. Singh is an innocent political victim. Others take it further. They call him "The Savior of Hinduism."[6]

In May 2005, the Orissa High Court suspended the death penalty. That determination has been appealed.

LIFE-AND-DEATH CONSEQUENCES

Staines's martyrdom was the stuff of faraway stories I heard as a child. I knew the world was as dangerous as ever. But now I came to terms with the fact that this call put us in the vortex of a movement of God that had serious life-and-death consequences. My respect and admiration for Dr. D'souza and his colleagues in ministry grew. Our partnership drew us into this world of risk. The horrific murder of Graham Staines and his two sons had a powerful impact on Joseph and his team in 1999. The intensity of these life stories heightened my spiritual awareness, focused my prayers, and strengthened the bonds of community. It was just an initiation, a start.

The assassination of a fifty-four-year-old missionary and his two boys was only the beginning of a terrible wave of violence that rolled over Orissa like a tsunami. The radical Dara Singh was implicated in several of the incidents. The martyring of a good man and his sons was reported around the world. The story galvanized all sides, increasing tensions and hostilities.

Many cite the destruction of the Babri Mosque in Ayodhya in 1992, in the northern district of the state of Uttar Pradesh by radical Hindu nationalists (their ideology called "Hindutva"). The mosque was one of India's largest in one of the most populous states where thirty one million Muslims live. When a gang of radical, fundamentalist Hindus leveled the Muslim place of pilgrimage, prayer, and worship, they believed they were redeeming the site for the Hindu world. Radicals have been emboldened ever since.

Atrocities against Christian workers are on the rise. And the Dalit people's suffering has only worsened.

Think of it this way. Dalits are considered slaves. They are expected to serve the upper castes. Their religion teaches that their plight in this life is a result of some awful crime committed in a former life. Their station in society is their destiny. To think of breaking out would be a violation of the rule of karma, the law of cause and effect, and any such breach in this life results in even further suffering in the next life. Fate has been cast. You are who you are: a slave. Your only hope is to accept this life, live it in obedience, and perhaps in the next life, you will do better.

The upper castes benefit from this system. Labor is performed at little or no cost. Certain necessary functions are considered ritually "impure." For example, in a country with virtually no system for the disposal of sewage, Dalits are expected to clear neighborhoods of human and animal waste. This role has been in place for thousands of years in a densely populated nation. Other impure occupations include butchery, leatherworks, the removal and disposal of dead animals, clearing latrines by hand, and handling rotting carcasses. All of these activities contaminate the worker, making him or her impure. Untouchable. For hundreds and hundreds of years, the assumption of separation, isolation, and distance remained firmly in place.

> Dalits are expected to clear neighborhoods of human and animal waste and other impure activities, all of which contaminate the workers, making them untouchable.

Until now.

Imagine visiting a pre–Civil War plantation and calling together those slaves laboring in the fields for a little meeting near the barn and suggesting to them that they are better than this; that they are made in the image of God; that they are no different, in God's sight, than their master; that they ought to envision and pursue a better life.

Or imagine standing on the deck of a tall slave ship on the Gold Coast of Africa bound for the New World and declaring independence and freedom to the slaves in chains below deck.

Or imagine entering a village where Dalits have performed slave labor for centuries and announcing that the religion that put them in bondage no longer applies.

Be prepared for opposition. Freedom has a cost.

Dara Singh is one example of many who have attacked Dalits and their advocates. He is an archetype of the bigotry and cruelty that fuel vigilante forces. He was arrested and found guilty in the murders of Graham Staines and the boys. But it is not the only crime associated with him and his gang of thugs.

In 1996, a truck loaded with cattle, bound for a slaughterhouse in Calcutta, was attacked and set ablaze. The driver and his helper were killed. A short time later, another such truck was attacked and seven Muslims were badly beaten. One died. A banner hung from the charred remains of the truck the following day with the name *Bajrang Dal* (Singh's organization): a sign of conquest. There are at least nine other cases that have been formally filed against Dara Singh.

While it may seem that the attacks on Dalit freedom are nothing new in the sad history of the clash of cultures, it does not mean that atrocities such as these are any more acceptable. Cruelty toward the Dalit people has remained pervasive, open, widespread, and far too commonplace.

> Human trafficking, which is a worldwide curse, is common in Dalit communities.

To catalog the abuse over hundreds of years would require an entire library of books.

Human Rights Watch published a widely distributed study called "Broken People: Caste Violence against India's 'Untouchables.'" Here's a summary of their report: "Between 1994 and 1996, a total of 98,349 cases were registered with the police nation-wide as crimes against scheduled castes [Dalits]. Of these, 38,483 were registered under the Atrocities Act. A further 1,660 were for murder; 2,814 for rape; and 13,671 for hurt."[7]

Out of these statistics, the Dalit Freedom Movement was born.

As conversions rise, the atrocities continue. Sexual abuse is commonplace. Disputes are routinely settled by violence. Dalit families who believe they have no alternative, sell their children away, particularly their girls. Human trafficking, which is a worldwide curse, is common in Dalit communities.

The world was outraged when, in a disturbing scene from *Slumdog Millionaire*, they watched a heartless child-racketeer pour boiling oil into the eyes of an eight-year-old boy—because blind beggars earn more on the streets than sighted beggars. When Latika (Jamal's friend from the slums who became his love interest later in the same film) ends up in a house of prostitution, audiences were appalled. Some walked out of the theater.

But such is the fate of many Dalit children. They are sold for cash in the villages. Promises of a better life may bring some measure of comfort to parents who believe they have no alternative, but these are usually meaningless. The children usually emerge in the cities, owned by their captor or a second buyer, where they are exploited for child labor, street begging, or the burgeoning sex trade.

Hindu fundamentalists charge outsiders with coercion tactics. The freedom movement points to the guarantee of religious freedom in the Indian constitution. Critics accuse Christians and others, claiming that they are forcing Dalits to convert for self-serving reasons; bribing them with money and Western influence.

Udit Raj, that same month, made his defense to *Christianity Today*.

How can we force such a large number of people into any religion? The tyranny of the caste system is what forces these poor souls into Christianity and Buddhism. Dalits are lynched and raped and destroyed systematically. In the name of privatization, the administration is taking away their job reservations. For them, what's the point in being a Hindu anymore?[8]

In the center of the high-pitched public debate, frequently facing violent persecution and ongoing abuse, are the children. They are caught in the deadly crossfire—with heartbreaking regularity.

Learning all this, I could barely sit still.

NOTES

1. One tradition places the apostle Thomas in southern India in the first century.
2. Thomas Friedman Reporting, *The Other Side of Outsourcing*, The Discovery Channel documentary, June 3, 2004. Transcript at http://assets.soomo.org/ssc/transcripts/3.11Outsourcing.pdf.

3. As quoted in Manpreet Singh, "India: Despised Dalits Quit Hinduism. Find New Dignity in Christ," *Christianity Today*, December 9, 2002.
4. Such as the BJP (Bharatiya Janata Party), the RSS (Rashtriya Swayamsevak Sangh), and the VHP (Vishwa Hindu Parishad).
5. "Hindu Given Death for Killing Missionary," *New York Times*, September 23, 2003.
6. Krishnaprasad Adyanthaya, managing trustee of Sri Mookambika Temple in Kollur, Dakshina Kannada district, Karnataka said in July 2007: "Dara Singh, who burned Christian missionary Staines at Orissa few years ago, is a role model to us. There are many Dara Singhs in Kundapur who can foil the attempt to convert." Several groups describe Singh as the "saviour of Hinduism," including Dharma-rakhyak Sri Dara Singh Bachao Samiti (Committee to Defend Dara Singh, the Protector of Our Religion) and Dara Sena (Dara's Army), claiming to espouse his cause.
7. "Broken People: Caste Violence against India's 'Untouchables,'" Human Rights Watch report, New York, 1999, p. 41.
8. Joshua Newton, "Police Arrest Indian Christians over Dalit Conversion," *Christianity Today*, December 1, 2002.

Chapter 7

PERSECUTION

THE GATHERING IN NEW DELHI on that day in November 2001 gave new impetus to Dalits hungering for liberation. Udit Raj's strategy to gather hundreds of thousands of Dalits in a mass demonstration of independence was frustrated at every turn. But in spite of calculated, ferocious opposition, it worked.

Absent government intervention, credible observers believe one million "untouchables" would have descended on India's capital in solidarity. As it was, overcoming all the odds, over one hundred thousand were determined enough to charge through the obstacles. Most of them joined in the renunciation of the system that has held them hostage for generations. But the impact of the mass conversion went far beyond New Delhi's B. R. Ambedkar Bhawan Stadium.

The bold stand taken by Udit Raj and articulated by Joseph D'souza and others unleashed a powerful spirit of renewal and infused confidence into the freedom movement. The lamp of hope was lit. It emboldened Dalits all over India. But the spark of change that was kindled also energized those who would extinguish the flame.

In January 2002, four months after the tens of thousands of Dalits had assembled in Bhawan Stadium, Dr. D'souza gave a dire prediction to an American magazine. "As some Hindu radicals feel this is a major assault on Hinduism, now I think there will be persecution of the Dalits." Then he added, "I wouldn't be surprised if there is persecution of Christians, too."[1]

Sadly, Dr. D'souza was right.

At the same time, Dalits all over India began to embrace their humanity. They understood the power of choice. Many were content to simply declare themselves non-Hindu. Others pursued Buddhism, some Islam. Many converted to Christianity, declaring themselves followers of Jesus, seeking baptism, discipleship, and membership in Christian churches.

But while India's constitution clearly permits the right to choose, for over sixty years that constitutional guarantee had been ignored or challenged. Anticonversion laws gained support. And violence against Christians did not stop with Graham Staines and his sons. The most vicious attacks targeted Dalit believers.

A GOD-SIZED CAUSE

I come from a place where personal comfort and security are paramount. Comfort is good when you need rest. But when it becomes a way of life, an end in itself, it breeds detachment, indifference, and mediocrity. We Christians who know nothing more than our manicured neighborhoods, our swept-up streets, our glittering shopping malls, our chrome-and-glass office buildings, our freeways that race us through the less-desirable communities in our cities, and our climate-controlled worship centers . . . well, we can miss it.

Miss what? In India I met believers for whom Christian fellowship is a vital lifeline. Prayer, a privilege and necessity. The Word of God, essential for spiritual nutrition. Worship that is vibrant and energetic. Jesus told His followers who were serious to pick up their cross. Maybe that is what we were missing. We had not associated ourselves with a God-sized cause. To do so involves a denial of self: a commitment to serve, even if it costs one's life.

In India, I was in the company of people willing to give their very lives to the cause of the Gospel. It had a profound impact on me.

For these folks, it is not an empty exercise or a dress rehearsal. It is real. I had an appetite to learn. I wanted to read. To study. To listen. I longed to know the stories of the heroes who were willing to stand strong in the face of direct, even violent opposition. I wanted to apprehend the power of God that is capable of overcoming the most heinous assaults of evil on good.

It all seemed so right in the courtyard of Uddamarri School, listening to the children singing with cheerful, smiling faces. But I would later come to understand the price that was paid for such a prize. I also knew that our vision would only be realized if there would be those willing to ante up and pay that price. It would transform a nation.

From my comfortable place back home, I knew such people were out there. Tears often filled my eyes as my heart responded to the real stories of endurance through persecution and loss. And yet even in the terrible tragedies, I understood how God made something beautiful and eternal rise out of the ashes of unspeakable evil.

I was about to learn the truth.

The British Broadcasting Corporation (BBC) reported in 2002 that police arrested ten people who were organizing a mass baptism to Christianity in Tamil Nadu, one of the primary states enforcing anticonversion laws. There were three thousand Dalits ready to convert. These arrests sparked protests all over the state.

Some of the Dalits who were converting to Christianity spoke out.

"I am very happy to become a Christian. I feel liberated, a human being," says A. Sekar. His eyes turn moist and his voice chokes with deep emotion. "I feel I am born again."

Sekar, 30, is a Dalit in Madurai, in India's southern Tamil Nadu state. Four members of his family of six have converted to Christianity in recent months.

Their Dalit neighbor, Ilaiyaraja, twenty-eight, has been going to the nearby Bethel Church to pray. "I've given notice to [the] church for baptism," Ilaiyaraja said. "Next month, I will be baptized. In Hinduism, you pray to a number of deities, while in Christianity there is only one God, which I feel is [the] original God. I find the Hindu caste system very inhuman and oppressive."[2]

These reports mobilized radical Hindus who would use every means possible to put a stop to the conversions. From the time of the mass event in New Delhi to the time I made the commitment to build Dalit schools, conversions multiplied, and so did the opposition.

Back in 2006, as I headed home with Brent and Mike and the others, we were filled with enthusiasm. Our vision of impacting a nation, eradicating the caste system that had suppressed millions for thousands of years, and building schools for Dalit children under the banner of Global Freedom, energized our thoughts. But I did not comprehend just how serious the opposition might be. As we flew back halfway across the globe, the stage was set for yet more hostility.

THE CHRISTMAS CONFRONTATION

Orissa, the state on the eastern coast of India bordering the Bay of Bengal, known for its staunch commitment to anticonversion laws, and the home of missionary martyr Graham Staines, stirred in anticipation of a wave of violence.

The murder of Staines and his two young sons stoked the tensions between a growing community of Christians (most of them Dalit) and the fundamentalist Hindus in the region. Christians were empowered and emboldened by the global outcry. Major media outlets from every continent reported the cruel and unprovoked assault on this gentle missionary.

Christian Dalits, in spite of the dangers, became more daring in their assertion of freedom.

Two days before Christmas, December 23, 2007, in the village of Brahmanigoan, a group of Christians boldly placed a large Christmas decoration (they called it a "Christmas gate") at the entrance of a Hindu temple. The provocative act stirred up a shouting match in the town square.

Brahmanigoan was home to Swamy Lakshamanananda Saraswati. Everyone knew him. Back in 1968, the swami left his wife and newborn son to pursue the life of a monk. Two years later, he started an ashram (a monastic community), and as the years passed, he immersed himself in the Hindutva philosophy. He believed in the purity of his religion, and that it was defiled by outside influences, especially from the corrupt, materialistic West. The three most damaging influences to Indian life, in his thinking, were communism, Islam, and Christianity. His determination to protect India from those three threats hardened. From his influential ashram, the swami taught everyone who would listen the doctrines of purity and resistance to invasions from the outside. He became a leading spokesman for the radical nationalist organization, the Vishwa Hindu Parishad (VHP).

When the swami heard about the Christmas ornament deliberately placed in defilement of the Hindu temple, he also received reports about the skirmish. He left his home and went directly to the temple where the noisy arguments attracted a crowd.

When he arrived, tempers flared. Shouting between those who believed in the freedom of the exercise of religion and those who were insulted by the appearance of a "Western" intrusion on this Hindu village escalated. Swamy Lakshamanananda joined in the debate. The Hindu crowd recognized his moral authority and stepped back, allowing him to take the imaginary platform. The shoving started. The debate turned into a brawl.

Suddenly, guns appeared. Enemies of the swami aimed their arms at him. And then, they assaulted him. No shots were fired.

But the swami was injured. He was eighty-two years old. The angry crowd dispersed, uttering epithets and threats from both sides. The Christmas confrontation was over.

> The word went out. Armed Christians were supposedly on the loose.

The word went out. Armed Christians were supposedly on the loose.

Tensions in Orissa had always been high. And now a new fuse was lit.

Orissa has been a center of Christian influence since Franciscan missionary Friar Odoric came to the territory back in the fourteenth century. When the British set up colonies all over India, Baptist Christian missionaries followed in the 1850s, close to the time of the American Civil War. Documents that survive that era speak of the fierce resistance of the Brahmins (Hindu priests) to Christian influence.

One hundred years later, after India won independence from British rule and established its own democratic constitution, Orissa enacted the Freedom of Religion Act of 1967. Its purpose was not so much to guarantee religious freedom as it was to make proselytizing illegal. If it could be shown that outsiders had unduly pressured folks to embrace their religion, they would be prosecuted.

In spite of attempts to silence the Christian message, the painful plight of the Dalits has been fertile soil for the Gospel. The good news brings a whole new worldview to oppressed Dalits. It speaks of a Creator who made Dalits in the image of the living God. It speaks of forgiveness, of redemption, of equal access. It also speaks of empowerment and opportunity. And it speaks of eternal certainty. The Christian message has been well received in Orissa in the Dalit community. Christianity is a liberating alternative to casteism.

Yet Christians are not the only group in India that opposes the caste system. There are many who claim to represent the untouchables of India, whether they are called Dalits or "Scheduled Castes" or "Scheduled

Tribes," which is the government's official way of identifying outcastes.

As a Hindu, the swami himself believed he was committed to the well-being of the Dalits. So does a radical faction calling themselves "Maoists," who believe they are working on behalf of the Dalits as a classically exploited class. Maoists base their philosophy on the teachings of Mao Zedong, whose revolutionary strategy for China was rooted in the teachings of Vladimir Lenin and Joseph Stalin. It is a Marxism that justifies violence in the pursuit of revolution against the ruling class. After a protracted struggle, Mao succeeded in taking control of China in 1949.

The Maoist philosophy and violent political strategy has inspired some Indian activists. Maoists in India believe that the revolution began by Chairman Mao is still spreading. Some studied the radical Black Panther Movement in the United States. They embrace violence as a legitimate means of tearing down the barriers between the oppressed and the oppressor, and are determined to bring revolution to India through acts of terror and brutality.

> The Christian message has been well received in Orissa's Dalit community. Christianity is a liberating alternative to casteism.

Some of those Maoist activists were in the crowd that fateful December 23 when Christians celebrated the birth of Jesus at the entrance to the Hindu temple in Brahmanigoan. The now infamous 2007–2008 persecution of Christians in the state of Orissa gathered deadly momentum.

DEATH OF A SWAMI

The wounded swami filed a formal complaint and won police protection. He also filed a grievance regarding the buying and selling of beef, an incendiary charge. He claimed that Christians profited from this illegal activity, killing cows, eating the meat, and selling the hides in a clear violation of Hindu law. Rumors flared with stories of attacks by Christians on Hindu homes.

Hindu radicals went on the rampage. The government sent in 2,500 police officers to restore order. Twelve hundred Dalits were forced from their homes and displaced into refugee camps.

For those weeks and then months afterward, the swami claimed he was the target of death threats. Local police took those threats seriously and posted armed guards on the ashram compound. The swami's speeches became increasingly bold. He denounced the activities of Christian missionaries and ministries. He made impassioned orations underscoring the necessity of the anticonversion laws. But his greatest disdain was reserved for the Maoist activists in the area—those outspoken and politically minded terrorists who believed that bloodshed is not only justified but necessary as a political and social tactic. He called for an end to Maoist atrocities.

> Christians were named as the perpetrators of the vicious crime.

In response, the organization's most violent group, the Maoist People's Liberation Guerrilla Army, targeted the local region. The swami sought to expose them. In his mind, they were as treacherous as the Christians.

On August 23, 2008, eight months after the Christmas confrontation, a swarm of thirty to forty men, faces covered, surrounded the ashram. They were heavily armed. The invaders bound and gagged the government's uniformed guards, who were useless protection. The masked thugs called out the aging yet defiant Swamy Lakshamanananda. With the use of two AK-47s and several handguns, the assassins gunned down the eighty-two-year-old Hindu swami, one of the VHP's most articulate proponents, in cold blood, as his young students watched in horror. Three of his organization's top lieutenants and a young boy were also shot and killed. Their mission accomplished, the gang of assailants vanished into the jungle.

Who were those masked killers? Speculation centered on the Christian community. First verbally, then in print, and finally radio and television reports: Christians were named as the perpetrators of the vicious crime.

Those same Dalit Christians who set up a Christmas ornament as an expression of freedom of religion were identified as the suspected executioners.

The rampage in Orissa began.

Notes

1. Joshua Newton, "Police Arrest Indian Christians over Dalit Conversion," *Christianity Today,* December 1, 2002.
2. Ibid.

Chapter 8

COMMUNITY

THE DALIT PEOPLE are not a metaphor.

The millions of untouchables in India, and in neighboring countries like Nepal, Bangladesh, and Pakistan, are real. They live and work and laugh and play and eat and sleep and love. They also suffer. They hurt for food and shelter from the cold and wind and rain. They are abused. Used.

For many of us, they exist in a faraway place, speak a strange language, and live in conditions that we would call unacceptable. We have seen photographs and video images. We have heard their voices and their musical, lyrical expression most likely through some sort of audio system. We see and hear the children squealing and laughing and watch them clamoring in front of someone's camera lens, but only by way of electronic media.

Some of us have been to India and walked up and down the makeshift rows of shanty towns, between the lean-to structures made of crooked poles and peeling plywood and corrugated aluminum sheets, with tattered canvas for walls and bare earth for floors. We may have played with the children and prayed with their mothers and fathers and grandparents. As we stroll through a place so unlike our own, we try to imagine such an existence. We may share a meal or even present gifts. But in the end, we walk away and return to our lives of comfort and excess.

Whether or not you have been there to meet Dalits personally, you should know this: these are real people. They are no metaphor or fiction. They are made in God's image, and they are the objects of His love. These are human beings. Each one has a name.

We share planet Earth. Our hearts go out to the Dalits, not in pity but in genuine affection. And as we stand and smile and attempt giddy, sometimes awkward conversation, often through a translator, their hearts go out to us, too. We can feel their love. They feel ours.

> Whether or not you have been there to meet Dalits personally, you should know this: these are real people.

I have been a pastor for many years. One of the most common remarks I hear from a fresh returnee from a mission trip is, "Pastor, I went thinking I was going to make an impact on them. But you know what? This is for real. *They* impacted me *far more* than *I* impacted them."

That comment comes in different forms, but the sentiment is the same. We go to serve. We go to listen. We go to give. We go to share. We bring a message of hope and encouragement. We bear witness to a Gospel that transforms. But ultimately, it is *our* world that gets turned upside down. Theirs stays pretty much the same.

"WHERE WERE YOU WHEN I WAS HUNGRY?"

After Jesus told a couple of metaphor-laden stories (sometimes called parables) to His followers, He pictured the day He would come back and establish His kingdom. He would hand out rewards and dole out judgments on that day. There were those who came to Him and made all sorts of inspiring claims about their work and selfless service. Jesus asked them a poignant question: "When I was hungry; when I was thirsty; when I was sick; in prison—where were you?"

"Jesus," they asked incredulously, "when were *You* hungry? When were *You* sick? When were *You* in prison?" They looked at each other in astonishment, as though they had missed the memo. "If we had only *known*, Jesus"—the gooey sincerity so thick it dripped—"we would have been there for You. No question about it."

> Here in India, for thousands of years, your caste is cast. Set in stone.

In Jesus' story, their self-serving claims sound hollow. Their perception of Jesus' identity and His purpose seem foggy. Their promise of loyalty and concern appear empty.

Then Jesus made a politically incorrect reference. He pointed to a group He called "the least of these."[1] On the surface, this may sound like a direct insult to a misunderstood minority. To whom does He refer?

As I wandered through the towns and villages and open slums in India and conversed with untouchables (the broken, the shattered, the outcastes, the Dalits), Jesus' words haunted me. "The least of these" is about as accurate a description of this people group as I could have invented. In my country, we are expected to see past race or station. In polite conversation, we assume equality, which is, according to the American Declaration of Independence, self-evident. But not so in India. Here, for thousands of years, your caste is cast. Set in stone. Immovable. Unchangeable. The "least of these." That is what you are.

So Jesus turns to His perplexed listeners and hits them with another piercing question. "When you encountered the hungry, the thirsty, the sick, the imprisoned . . . what was your response? What did you do?"

EXPOSED

And in a flash, these folks who had convinced themselves that they were prime candidates for a palatial estate in the foothills of Jesus' kingdom thought about it. They had immediate recall of those moments in time when they were indeed confronted with hunger and thirst and nakedness and injustice and want. In a flash of culpable insight, they recognized that in every case, they simply turned away. They moved quickly ahead with the business of the day. They left the hungry unfed. The thirsty without a drink. The sick with their aching stomachs and feverish foreheads and congested lungs and bloodshot, weeping eyes. And when they saw the one in prison, they turned away, thinking about how good it is to see the offender confined where he belongs and how thankful they were to not be in that cell. And these very thoughts themselves brought an awful condemnation. They missed it, and they knew it. Their master teacher nailed them with a piercing truth. They felt exposed.

Jesus was compelled to explain. It was a revelation. "If you will tend to the needy, just take the time to reach out with something of value in a spirit of kindness, you will be tending to Me."

It is an incredible thought, really. I have meditated on it over and over again, and it makes complete sense. When we reach out, in Jesus' name, to feed someone—to care for someone, to provide water, to stand up for injustice—in every case, *we meet Jesus there.*

When people inform me that on their mission trip they were impacted more than the people they went to help, I simply smile and remind them, yes indeed. *You met Jesus.* You touched the heart of God. You felt His very presence.

And when *that* happens, everything changes. Everything.

"WE HAVE A CASTE SYSTEM, TOO!"

Stay with me here. Because in another sense, the Dalits *are* a metaphor.

Please do not misunderstand. That does not make them any less real. The Dalits teach us something profound. Their message has universal application.

As she considered the plight of the Dalits, one of the college students at our church blurted out, "Hey! We have a caste system, too. Right here in Orange County!"

Well, not really. It would be a gross misrepresentation to suggest that our social stratification is tantamount to the horrors of casteism. But she did make an interesting and perhaps powerful point. Even in *our* churches, we measure a person's value by the size and location of their home, the make and model of their automobile, and the retail value of their wardrobe. We congregate in ways that betray our perceived status. We shun the needy down the street. Our language betrays prejudices and biases of which we are hardly aware.

> Now that I have made a serious commitment to the Dalits, I see my own neighborhood with a new set of eyes.

We as a congregation now worship in a large room. As I survey the crowd from weekend to weekend, I know many of the stories of the people who come to sing praise and pray and learn. While I do not know many who miss meals, I am aware of the enormous stresses and heartache that folks bring with them on any given Saturday or Sunday. There is a different kind of hunger and thirst, but both are heartrending. Many come afflicted with debilitating illness and mysterious diseases, and many are caught in a bondage that might as well be a prison house. They long for freedom.

In the next town over, there is a well-known neighborhood that is controlled by gangs. Thugs peddle sex and drugs. Fear reigns. Violence is all too common. Residents feel no safety.

America has become multicultural. In a changing economy, ethnicities and language groups multiply. Our young people are targeted with seductive marketing efforts that draw them away from home and family and their own dreams and aspirations. Money does not buy motivation. It does not guarantee mutual respect or family harmony.

Now that I have made a serious commitment to the Dalits, I see my own neighborhood with a new set of eyes. I listen differently. I have a new level of sensitivity to the needs of my own neighborhood. I have a new passion for the ministry of the Gospel in people's real lives.

It is as though I met Jesus. Where? In that awful slum, where I met the hungry, the sick, the disenfranchised. The victims of the unspeakable abuse of human trafficking. The slum, where hopelessness reigned. It happened when I met with "the least of these." I offered myself in simple obedience. And now that I think about it, He was there. When I got myself to that place I never imagined I would be, I discovered that these are not the "least of these" after all. They are human beings with hopes and longings and heart. It is not that Jesus misspoke. As usual, He made a powerful, penetrating point. In His own way, He got me there. And then He met me, just as He said He would.

I developed a new appetite. I wanted more.

BRINGING GLOBAL FREEDOM HOME

And so, our strategy for serving Jesus among the Dalits of India unfolded. The specifics came into focus. Back when we were in the planning stages for a new worship center in Yorba Linda, California, I considered it "Phase One." Once that first phase was complete, we understood that it was time to lay the groundwork for our second phase. There were several elements in the plan. We knew we needed to improve our existing facility, needed to address deferred maintenance issues. We were longtime partners in an accredited private school that has served our community with distinction since 1975, offering classes in kindergarten through eighth grade. We were committed to expanding that program to twelfth grade. The dream of a high school would be a major undertaking.

> What we learned in India had relevance in our hometown.

For this second phase, we looked for an outward focus. It made no sense for us to remain comfortable. It was undeniable. I had found the vision for Global Freedom that night back in the Corporate Stay Hotel.

Global Freedom: the essence of the Gospel message. It stirs in the hearts of nearly 300 million forgotten people in India, whether they see it or not. That longing for freedom is real. And that same longing stirs us right here at home, too.

As we mapped out our strategy, we understood that our focus on the other side of the globe needed to be balanced by a focus on needs in our own backyard. What we learned in India had relevance in our hometown.

With a new understanding of mission, I pulled together our team. I challenged them to think broadly about the implications of Global Freedom right here in Orange County, California. I asked them to connect their mission and

> The buildings have purpose only if real transformation is happening. Bricks and mortar support the expansion of spiritual development.

vision to the broad scope of Global Freedom. I explained something of the plight of the Dalit people of India, the hopelessness and systemic oppression. But the Gospel brings a message of hope and redemption. It affirms the value of every person made in the image of God. People are not looking for religion. This is not an exercise in comparative religion or the dominance of one culture over another. It is, rather, a transformation from the inside out.

In the transformation, a new community emerges. Character and integrity become the hallmarks of this new life. It opens the door to learning. It is more than progress for the sake of progress; more than profits to fatten up bank accounts. It gives birth to a whole new view of the world.

The Dalits of India are responding to this message. It is God's work in the world. It is happening over there. I challenged our team to imagine what it looks like when it happens over here.

This new phase would involve bricks and mortar. But the buildings have purpose only if real transformation is happening. Bricks and mortar support the expansion of spiritual development. So how can our plans contribute to this pursuit of Global Freedom?

It surprised me. First, I was astonished as I listened to myself. I am not quite sure where this compelling message came from—it flowed so easily. The words came naturally. It was as though my whole life experience prepared me for this moment in time. Unlike so many of my responsibilities in the past, this one was no chore. The enthusiasm was not contrived or manufactured. The conviction was not forced. I have heard people talk about inspiration, when God mysteriously breathes something of Himself into the creative process. And that's what it felt like. Too often, well-meaning folks mistakenly use God to sanction their own flimsy arguments or to justify their poor choices and thereby make a direct challenge impossible. What I experienced had nothing to do with using God to bolster my weak position. It had everything to do with the simple telling of a powerful story I had witnessed myself. It is God's story, not mine. And what flowed out felt like rivers of living water. I couldn't stop the flow.

Second, I was pleasantly surprised at our team's response. They did not react as though I was burdening them with just one more unwelcome assignment. Instead, the lights turned on. They made the connection. They seemed to understand that when I told the story of the Dalit people on the other end of the world, I was telling something of the story of their own ministries. On every level, they could see their own mission statements as a part of the whole.

So my enthusiasm and our team's response made for a potent mix. I could see new energy for what might otherwise might become routine, predictable, and bland.

DOWN ON CYPRESS STREET

The real starting point was Cypress Street, in the next town over, not even three miles away from my office.

In August that year, our county's major regional newspaper blazed a headline that caught all of our attention: "Yorba Linda Is Richest U.S. City."

The opening lines explained, "Don't bother counting Beemers and Range Rovers. Don't even look for the priciest houses. America's highest-income city is Yorba Linda." Apparently, the US Census Bureau determined that our little town tucked away in North County had the highest average per household income in the nation. We were even ahead of Newport Beach, the paper said.

And yet, three miles away from my office is a section of town that is unsafe. Families crowd into what little housing is available. Unemployment is high. There are language barriers. Children are left to wander. Drug trafficking rules the streets. The crime rate soars way above the average. Educational resources are limited, substandard.

All over Southern California, there are neighborhoods, like Cypress Street, that are neglected. In India, the Christian church has acquiesced to the caste system for generations, and has remained shamefully silent. In the United States, the church has earned a reputation for making eleven o'clock Sunday morning the most segregated hour of the week. I have often wondered how Jesus' words stack up against our neglect.

But something was happening on Cypress Street. It began when our high school and college students sponsored a Vacation Bible School right in the middle of town. Our students came back with a great vision. When our team came together, we could see the work that was expanding right around the corner was a part of God's heart for Global Freedom. I could see it in their eyes and hear it in their voices. Their story motivated our entire team.

What happened next still amazes me. For so many years, as a pastor, I found myself in the position of persuader, trying to convince people to move from lethargy to action. From inward to outward, from miserliness to generosity. And when my efforts failed to stimulate a high level of productivity, I slipped into dark periods of discouragement, thinking only of my ineffectiveness. But now, energy for ministry seemed to be released everywhere, apart from my direct involvement.

What began as a summer outreach to Cypress Street in the La Jolla district of our neighboring town has become a full-orbed, transformational ministry to an entire community. We now call it LOT318. "Loving Others in Truth," from the first epistle of John in the Bible. It has expanded. Our people share this commitment: "To empower a new generation of at-risk young people to understand their worth and pursue their God-given potential."

When our team connected the dots and linked LOT318 to our efforts in India, we began to grasp the power of Global Freedom. We understood that this new initiative in our second phase of expansion would be inspired by the transformation we witnessed firsthand in the slums of India. It would be our Community Impact thrust, which would involve our people in local outreach with the same energy, focus, and zeal we had witnessed halfway around the world.

We also understood that partnership would be essential to our strategy. Our team pulled together other organizations that up until this point had an unofficial connection to our ministry. We proposed that we get more serious about uniting our efforts, sharing resources, expanding awareness, and building on the transforming power of the Gospel through cooperative effort.

LOT318 set the pace. It now has a high profile on Cypress Street, hosting movie nights and soccer nights and home Bible studies. There are regular field trips and tutoring classes (many of them one-on-one) and even outreaches to the local senior care center. Every Sunday, a shuttle picks up a busload of children and adults and gets them to our campus for worship. People tell me that in five years, the whole community has been transformed. And it is only beginning.

THE "BEAUTIFUL MESS" OF WORKING TOGETHER

In the process, we have connected to a community development organization founded by a group of college students in the next town. They

Students welcoming the team
from Friends Church at the Good
Shepherd School in Chittoor, India.
(photo: Stephen Martin)

Dalit family at Pipe Village, Hyderabad, India. (photo: Stephen Martin)

above: Students praying for their lunches at the Good Shepherd School in India. (photo: Stephen Martin)

left: Matthew Cork posing for a picture with a student in a Good Shepherd School classroom in India. (photo: Jon Costley)

above: Exterior of a Dalit
home at Pipe Village,
Hyderabad, India.

right: Interior of a Dalit
home at Pipe Village,
Hyderabad, India.

below: Pipe Village,
Hyderabad, India.
(photos: Stephen Martin)

Young boy in a slum in India. (photo: Albert Russell)

above: Ken Kemp at Pipe Village.

right: from left:
Andrew Wolgemuth, Ken Kemp,
Stan Leach, and Kay Gadd
welcomed at Good
Shepherd School.

(photos: Ken Kemp)

Persis Karen (Annika)—actress and real-life student.
(photo: Ken Kemp)

above: Matthew Cork and Joseph D'souza attending a celebration at the Operation Mobilization main campus in India.

right: Friends Church staff members Jay Hoff, Matthew Cork, and Brent Martz with friend Kumar Swamy. (photos: Jon Costley)

above: On location on a busy street in India.

left: Matthew Cork and Dr. Joseph D'souza talking with women rescued from the sex trade in India.

(photos: Albert Russell)

above: *Not Today* stars
Cody Longo and Walid Amini
on location in India.

right: Matthew Cork and
Dr. Joseph D'souza on the
set of *Not Today*.
(photos: Albert Russell)

left: Storyboard of Persis Karen (Annika) running scene.

below: Crew filming *Not Today* on location in a slum in India.
(photo: Albert Russell)

above: *Not Today* star
Cody Longo on location
in India.

right: Storyboard of
India train scene.

Series of stills from movie.

above: Boy reading in his classroom at a Good Shepherd School in India.

left: Girls reading at a Good Shepherd School in India.

below: Dalit students in prayer at a Good Shepherd School in India.
(photos: Stephen Martin)

Not Today stars Cody Longo and
Walid Amini meet with students in India.
(photo: Albert Russell)

Boy reading in his classroom at a
Good Shepherd School in India.
(photo: Stephen Martin)

share our vision and our purpose. In partnership with their organization, Solidarity, our activities have broadened to include after-school programs in at-risk communities that focus on sports and tutoring—body and mind. Solidarity brings families and school officials together to solve problems and strengthen relational bonds. Kids focus on reading, writing, and math, the basics foundational to future success.

Along the way, we brought in an organization called Birth Choice. The risk of early pregnancy in our sexually charged culture is high. Birth Choice exists to aid women surprised by pregnancy. Its staff provides access to medical professionals and acts as advocates in navigating what can be an intimidating system. At whatever stage, Birth Choice is there, with prayer and counseling. There is support for recovery postabortion. Help with child care, and infant care for new mothers. Supplies and health care for young mothers without insurance or other resources.

We selected another Global Freedom partner, Habitat for Humanity. We are currently committed to building four affordable homes here in our neighborhood. A good number of our folks have volunteered.

It is a sad reality—many in our community are shortsighted. They believe homelessness is a problem for law enforcement. We believe otherwise. Every Saturday morning, a crew from our church gets up early to staff up, prepare, and serve a hot meal for our county's homeless folks.

Mary McAnena was eighty-two years old when she served the first meal to the needy in 1984. When she died in 2003, she was one hundred years old. But her compassion and care inspired many to reach out. Meals have been available to Orange County's hungry since then, and our folks have been active as regular volunteers. We call Mary's Kitchen a "beautiful mess" and it is an official Global Freedom partner.

Our young people have a history of serving on the staff of Calicinto Ranch, located out in the country. The Ranch exists to provide the children of incarcerated parents a place for support and guidance and care. Society is unkind to these children, who are often forgotten and mistreated and burdened with the fear that their future has been taken away by the misdeeds of their parents. Calicinto Ranch has a long record of breaking the cycle that condemns too many of these children. By giving them exposure to the world of ranching, responsibility to care for and exercise a horse, and all the chores associated with the property, in the context of skilled counselors and hours filled with meaningful activities, transformation happens.

> Our recovery ministries knew their efforts to combat addictions and help people free themselves from abusive relationships were as urgent as freeing India's Dalits.

Enthusiasm mounted as our team brought vision and direction to our Global Freedom cause from all parts of our church family. It came from our children's ministry team. Students developed fund-raising projects and outreach that matched our vision. Our Community Groups, our worship and arts team, our men's and women's organizations, all of them, lined up behind Global Freedom's aim. Our volunteers stepped up. Our recovery ministries understood that their efforts to combat addictions and help people free themselves from destructive obsessions and abusive relationships were just as urgent and timely as freeing India's Dalits. They all understood that we are called to action in Jesus' name.

And as our own enthusiasm grew, our list of partners grew. Out of both joy and tragedy, people wanted to make a difference in the lives of those around them.

TRAGEDY AND HOPE

Back in May of 2005, we got the terrible news. One of our congregation's own, fourteen-year-old Amber Craig, took her own life. Self-destructive behavior, especially among young people, is endemic in our nation. Our community is not exempt. Amber's death was a painful tragedy that left parents, friends, schoolteachers, administrators, coaches, and pastors with unanswered questions and aching grief. As the reality of Amber's tragic, irreversible choice settled in, an outpouring of support resulted in the creation of The Amber Craig Memorial Foundation. Out of that response, "With Hope" was born as a state-of-the-art suicide prevention center. It exists to be available, provide information, promote community awareness, and offer hope to families, schools, and churches who have nowhere else to turn.

Our recovery team has built a diverse collection of support groups for people who combat sex, food, and chemical addictions, as well as dysfunctional relationships that yield to abuse and codependency. They also got involved, knowing that their participants are longing to be free. The chains that bind them to their addictions can be broken. Their attendance at our meetings is their own declaration of independence from those damaging dependencies; but they need support. They get it. As they take a stand against the obsessions so common in our culture, they are as much a part of Global Freedom as are Dalits who renounce casteism.

Perhaps more than most, our folks in recovery identify with our friends in India—Dalits who have found hope and a future in following Jesus.

THE VISION THAT GIVES LIFE

As the Global Freedom story began to unfold at home, I found myself repeating the same passage from the book of Proverbs my parents taught me when I was young that I had murmured to myself while I was in India on that first trip: "Where there is no vision, the people perish."

When we lose sight of God's work in the world, something dies within us. If we lose contact with the heartbeat of God, if we no longer see the hope for restoration, the passion against injustice, the grief for those who are victimized by the devastating forces of evil and destruction, if we lose sight of the power of the Word of God to remedy what is wrong, as a people, we perish.

It is a strong word: *perish.* We say that food is perishable because it spoils. If it is left unconsumed, out in the open air, it deteriorates. It goes beyond uselessness. It can become toxic. Eat rotten food and your body will suffer. When people perish, they have lost their sense of purpose, their sense of usefulness. They lose the capacity to effect change. They no longer solve problems. In fact, they can become toxic. As the well-known Christian philosopher Francis Schaeffer said, they fall below the "line of despair."

The prophet Amos predicted a famine. But he was clear, not a shortage of food or water. It would be a severe drought of God's living Word. The damage would be even greater than the absence of nutrition or hydration. It would be a terrible withering away of the spirit.

I have studied that proverb about vision in other translations. In them, vision is connected to the revelation of God's presence and voice. It often came through the prophets. The account of the history of the people of Israel records several periods when that revelation was nowhere to be found. These were spiritual dry spells for the nation. People were lost. Confused. They were vulnerable to the influence of foreign ways.

> A severe drought of God's living Word causes damage even greater than the absence of nutrition or hydration —a terrible withering away of the spirit.

The proverb is sometimes translated this way: they "cast off restraint." We might say, they just didn't care anymore. "Whatever" became a byword. A theme. "Who cares?" "What's the point?" "So what?" "No one will know." Every expression you can imagine that dismisses us from responsibility, that numbs our conscience, that justifies our indulgences, that eliminates our fear of consequence, all of them are used in abundance when we "cast off restraint."

In other words, we perish. Spiritually, we die.

Religion is all around us. There are houses of worship everywhere. All over the world, people give expression to their spiritual nature, their curiosity about transcendence. Much of what we call religion is little more than ritual. It is an obligatory repetition of traditional motions that people hope will have some sort of merit in the long run. But if that is the sum of it, then no wonder religion has such little impact. I, for one, have no interest in that bland brand of religiosity.

If religion is not simply a ritual, then too often (and worse), it is a fraudulent excuse to rally people around spurious causes. We see the abuse of religion in the perpetration of crimes against humanity. It triggers war. It justifies random violence. It is inexcusable. It angers me.

God is not impressed with religion. He seeks us out for *relationship*.

He reveals Himself. We either see it, or we don't. That is the power of vision—a vision of Him.

So vision is essential. And I saw it at work with my own eyes among our leadership as we launched our Global Freedom campaign. As we pulled our team together around our commitment to building schools for Dalits in India, we were connecting with the powerful revelation of God's redeeming work. It bolstered our belief. It energized our planning. It galvanized our conviction.

If absence of vision leads to spiritual death, then the presence of vision brings life. And that is what I saw in the eyes and heard in the voices of our leadership.

Three adverbs came to my mind as I considered all this. As this vision took hold of us and then spread through every level of our organization, three dynamics were clearly in play. We proceeded *patiently*, *collaboratively*, and *progressively*.

Patiently. It took five full years to move the congregation from church split to a global vision. It required considerable patience. But in the end, it resulted in commitments totaling millions of dollars and untold numbers of volunteer hours.

Collaboratively. While I had something of a Sinai experience of my own (back there at the Corporate Stay Hotel in Bangalore), the revealed vision was still incomplete. God called us to a process. In its original conception, the overall vision was compelling but partial. During a sustained period of incubation and input, I included a wide range of participants to craft the overall vision, clarify the detail, and fill in the gaps. Over time, often painstaking, the vision emerged in its present form. It is important to understand that I did not mandate a fully developed, preconceived vision. That never would have worked. Rather, the vision was created in the context of a deliberate, intentional process of teamwork. This is how God works. This collaboration was essential if our people would ultimately buy in and take ownership.

Progressively. Over those five years, my primary role was to move people steadily toward that emerging vision. Everything we did was designed to make progress toward that goal, one step at a time.

As I see it now, our plan required all three elements. It took patience. It required collaboration. We moved progressively. We embraced God's vision for us, and it became our own. His plan, our plan. His heart, our heart.

When we see God in action, and we become a part of His plan to bring hope to the hopeless, help to the helpless, a cup of cold water to the thirsty, a loaf of bread for the hungry, literacy to the illiterate, empowerment against unbeatable odds, when we line up with all of that, we meet Him. When it happens corporately, together we are changed.

The Dalits are no metaphor. They are real. We learn from them. Their transformation has reawakened something in us that transforms us, too.

Our church nearly perished. I nearly perished. We lost our way. We lost our vision. Then, by the unmerited grace of God Almighty, our vision was restored, and the improbable became probable.

We would make a movie.

NOTE

1. Matthew 25:40, 44–46.

Chapter 9

NOT TODAY

BY NOW, OUR ENTIRE CHURCH was catching the vision. We introduced our people to Dr. D'souza. We sent several teams to India. I stepped up my efforts to read books, including Joseph's first: *Dalit Freedom: Now and Forever.* All of our experiences simply confirmed what we believed from the start.

The story is so big, so compelling that most everyone who took the time to try and understand became convinced right along with us. It was a calling. There was and is an urgency to this call. We all sensed it. People are suffering. And as we learned from the Orissa violence, people are dying. It is time to stop the abuse. We can end it—but we need to mobilize. We need action. We need focus.

Our new facility attracted a whole new level of expertise and professionalism. Our global vision unleashed a tidal wave of creative energy. Writers wanted to write. Musicians composed songs. Videographers and editors and photographers launched new initiatives to capture images.

THE MAKING OF "DELETES"

Brent Martz, our pastor of creative ministries, wanted to know more. He took his film crew to India, prepared to ask questions. He brought along Jon Van Dyke, our on-staff media director. They met with our local partners, toured slums, and studied the situation for Dalits in India in considerable depth. When they came home, they had plenty of filmed and recorded data. They were as deeply moved by what they saw as I was. They went to work on a documentary short.

They called it "Deletes."

It is a curious wordplay. To be deleted is to be eliminated, to cease to exist. It can be a computer file, or it can be hundreds of millions of human beings. Delete.

Like a Dalit.

> It was as though our entire congregation had been to the slums of India and spoken to the forgotten Dalits themselves.

Our team recognized that a whole class of people has been systematically deleted from any cultural or social standing. Their value, their needs, their access to human development has been dispatched into nothingness by a system that has been firmly in place for thousands of years. Deleted as though they do not exist, except to perform degrading, debasing services that confirm their lowly place in the scheme of things. Their mere presence in the company of the upper caste is strictly prohibited.

As Brent and Jon poured themselves into their work, they created a powerful, compelling piece. In sight and sound, they got it. We showed their video to our people. It brought our whole vision into focus. It made us feel, it informed our minds, it touched our hearts. It was as though our entire congregation had been to the slums of India and spoken to the forgotten Dalits themselves.

Their work got early recognition from Hollywood filmmakers. It gave us a taste of what could be done if we simply focused our energies and resources.

In the fall of 2006, a full-length feature film made the rounds in theaters across America. I had been invited to promote the film among our people, but frankly, I did not pay it much attention then. It was one of many hundreds of promotions that come across my desk on a regular basis. The movie was called *Facing the Giants*.

What I did not know at the time was that the film was made entirely by a local church just outside Atlanta. A group of talented people got together and affirmed that one of the most effective ways to influence a generation is the movie theater.

I was inspired by the story of Sherwood Baptist Church. So were Brent and Jon. As we looked at the landscape of our own talent pool, we realized that we were blessed with all the resources that would make a full-length feature film possible.

The idea first came to me in the form of an email from my friend and coauthor Ken Kemp, who proposed the wild idea of a dramatic film. It was one of those "aha" moments educators talk about. That same day, Brent stepped into my office. I read Ken's email. Brent laughed out loud; he literally had a stack of storyboards under his arm. Turns out, his team had been planning . . . a movie. A drama. A full-length feature film for the theaters. That very day, they strategized on how to bring the idea to me without being laughed out of the room. He came ready to share their ideas for a movie. We'll never forget that first discussion around the new idea. It was filled with energy and excitement and can-you-believe-this enthusiasm.

WE WANT THE WORLD TO KNOW

First of all, we knew that we had an extraordinary story to tell. We also believed that while a documentary could be powerful, a dramatic story has even greater potential to impact lives, connect emotionally, and inspire action. We talked a lot about this new generation known for its preference for story over sermon. This wired generation, where connectivity is a way of life, engages naturally with character and drama and comedy and dialogue. Sherwood Baptist got it right. Their success inspired us.

So we got serious about the possibilities. I encouraged our creative arts team, led by Brent and Jon, to think big.

The world needs to understand that slavery still exists. Even today, young children are bought and sold like trinkets. Little girls are forced into the dark, illicit sex trade. Young boys and girls are coerced to beg in the streets, and bring their proceeds back to line the pockets of thugs who abuse them at night. Others are forced into labor mills with long hours, intolerable heat, and strict production quotas, all in horrible working conditions, cutting the young away from any possibility of education. The dark streets of the swarming city become a marketplace where young adolescents are offered for sale to satisfy the base needs of amoral souls who think nothing of the lifelong impact of a few reckless minutes.

> Even today, young children are bought and sold like trinkets.

Meanwhile, parents, who are generally illiterate and caught in a deadly cycle of poverty, are too easily convinced by brokers of child slavery that the transaction is in everyone's best interest. Cash in hand, a Dalit slum-dweller relents. The child leaves the village in the company of a heartless middleman on his way to market where he will sell off his new acquisition at a sizeable markup. The impact on India is enormous; the human toll, unthinkable. The shadowy underworld of human trafficking victimizes millions of Dalits every year.

With our own eyes, we have seen the contrast: how the message of hope transforms. How education derails the evil intent of traffickers for whom profits trump decency. We want the world to know. We are compelled to get the message out.

So we entertained the daring notion that a full-length feature film could touch millions—and mobilize folks who are looking to make their lives count.

At first, it was a simple "what-if." What if we take the resources we use to produce our weekend services and direct them toward the production of a full-length film? What if we unleash our talented writers? Camera crews? Lighting directors? Sound engineers? Actors? Musicians? What if?

The more we talked, the more convinced we were that we could do it.

SLUMDOG OPENS THE DOORS

What we did not anticipate was the appearance of that little independent film turned Oscar winner, *Slumdog Millionaire*. Curiously, the slick, high-energy film emerged as a contender for Best Picture just as we were kicking around the idea of our own motion picture. We never thought of it as competition. We heard from industry people that a hit movie that dealt with the issues of casteism in India would only create more interest in our project.

It turned out to be true.

The first thirty minutes of *Slumdog Millionaire* take the viewer into the murky world of slum life, so prevalent all over the world's second most populous nation. The scenes are disturbing enough to give the film an "R" rating. Polite Indian society objected to the film. They feared that such exposure might slow the nation's progress in attracting business from around the world. Ironically, the Dharavi slum in Mumbai, where the movie was filmed, is now a popular, though controversial tourist attraction.

> Major studios now understand that there is a significant audience for faith-based motion pictures.

But the film became unstoppable. While it fell short of exploring the problem in greater depth, it has opened doors.

Other films, like the *Passion of the Christ* and *Facing the Giants* and *Fireproof*, have established that films with a potent Christian message are viable in the marketplace. Major studios now understand that there is a significant audience for faith-based motion pictures. They have established divisions, certainly not for the advancement of any particular religious group, but to serve an audience and generate profits for their shareholders. I welcome this development. We saw it all coming together. Preparedness and opportunity were about to intersect.

The concept of *Not Today* was born.

Not Today became the working title of the film project that is central to our Global Freedom vision. (Our first title was *Open Wide Your Heart*.) Brent and Jon sketched out a story line. I sent them away for a couple of weeks to hammer out a complete script. They came up with a powerful story.

TO RESCUE ANNIKA

Their script describes a young, cynical, privileged, recent college graduate. One night he plays a hand in a poker game with his fraternity pals. They are bored, looking for something to break the predictable routines, young enough to launch out on a random adventure yet old enough to go anywhere in the world. The combination of a destiny-charged poker hand and the toss of a dart thrown over the shoulder at a map of the globe both come together. The fraternity brothers eventually wind up in central India.

There the young man, Caden Welles, encounters a young girl with black eyes and black flowing hair, a tattered dress, and a winning smile. She touches her lips and then her stomach, signaling hunger, and then opens her hand. She and her father work the American for a handout.

Caden is taken by the plight of this little girl. He later learns her name: Annika. He gives her some pocket change. He wonders where she lives and where she eats. Does she attend school? In an intriguing circumstance, he then befriends her father, Kiran Maruthi. Caden is introduced to the slum world Annika and her father call home.

The script takes Caden on a wild ride, tossing his emotions back and forth—from rage to terror to laughter to love to fear to hope and to despair—and back around again. Social and economic pressures leave her father little choice. Young Annika gets caught in the sordid underworld of trafficking. A quintessential ugly American, Caden has no spiritual resources, no altruistic calling, but when he learns of Annika's fate, he leaves everything behind, obsessed with her rescue. The rescue attempt takes him on a journey through India's dark corners, crammed slums, long trains, "sacred" rivers polluted with human ash and animal waste, through byways and alleyways where street corruption goes unchecked.

His girlfriend and his mother pray for him from the safety of their homes in Southern California. He is annoyed by their religiosity. But the quest to rescue and liberate a little girl with bright eyes and an engaging smile and bring her home to her father becomes his life's mission. And a young man who until now believed he had it all is torn by tension and turmoil in his soul.

The team completed the first version of the script. For Brent and Jon, it was a life-changing process. They made a trip to Hyderabad. There they saw Pipe Village and visited several Dalit schools. They talked to teachers and community leaders. They met the parents of the young students. They walked through slums in several cities. They caught the contrast. The story they created for the movie flowed from that experience.

The first version of the script complete, it was time for them to return. They would validate their impressions, scope out filming locations, build relationships with people in India who could help with permissions and assist them in navigating on-location filming.

The team prepared for a second trip.

THE POLICEMAN WHO WEPT

Dr. Prakash Anantha (name changed for security purposes) is a close friend of Dr. D'souza. For years, he worked as a police officer in Hyderabad. As a follower of Jesus, he had a special sensitivity to one of the most prevalent categories of crimes in his state of Andra Pradesh: human trafficking.

It became his primary focus. A law enforcement officer with too much street experience, he wrote a doctoral dissertation on the subject. It earned him a PhD.

He is the father of three and an active lay minister. He also travels all over India speaking to educators, political leaders, law enforcement officials, medical professionals, and the business community about the widespread criminal activity that is pervasive throughout Asia, but is an acutely thorny problem in India. While prostitution is technically illegal, the problem is so enormous, so entrenched in the culture, so much a part of the economy, so deftly controlled by powerful crime organizations that law enforcement can only respond to specific complaints. The street business thrives, virtually unchecked.

> Day or night, the sex trade thrives. When a girl is violated, she becomes worthless.

Prakash Anantha is passionate about reform. He and a growing number of political and social activists are demanding action. The International Justice Mission calls human trafficking "the fastest growing enterprise in the world." In India alone, some thirty million men, women, and children are caught in the web, "enslaved by violence."

Anantha traveled with our film crew. He introduced them to the vile world of human trafficking, from the city dump in Hyderabad, to the slums of Bangalore, and on up to Calcutta (also known as Kolkata) via a passenger train, into the heart of the crowded city so ravaged by years of economic ruin since the colonial era when the city sparkled—Calcutta, the home of Mother Teresa, who dedicated her life to nursing the dying. Then the team went on to Mumbai. They toured the red-light districts of those large cities, and saw the long, narrow streets where prostitutes welcome their customers openly. Pimps lure paying guests and guide inquirers to find what they are seeking.

Our team witnessed the pervasive presence of *young* girls, well underage. Children wait with their mothers as couples disappear into the shadows down the halls. Day or night, the sex trade thrives. When a girl is violated, she becomes worthless. No one will take her as a bride. She is an untouchable untouchable. Her life, her hopes, her aspirations, her dreams are carelessly snatched from her. And yet, thoughtless married men line up at the open doors along with their single counterparts, apparently indifferent to the damning consequences of their actions, ready to pay cash. If they are not indifferent, they are calloused.

It calls up a line from the powerful stage play and recent movie based on the Victor Hugo novel *Les Miserables*. In Paris, in the turbulent early 1800s, Fantine turns to prostitution in a futile attempt to save her daughter, Cosette. In anguish, she poses a haunting question when she sings, "Don't they know they're making love to one already dead?"

Dr. Anantha, a Dalit orphan, educated and spiritually reborn, has made a career out of rescuing these girls.

If a trafficked girl caught in the sex trade simply asks, state officials are empowered to remove her from the brothel and deliver her to a recovery center. It is the law. But the young women who seek freedom, all too often return to the streets. There are few who will help them overcome the stigma and stain of violated lives. Dr. Anantha often weeps as he tells the story. When he considers the plight of these young women, emotion gets the best of this veteran law enforcement official.

Human trafficking targets Dalits. Many children are sold directly into the sex trade. Some are delivered to "adoption agencies." Some get caught in the despicable but growing human organ trade where vital organs are bought and sold on the black market. Many of these children do not survive the forced, illicit surgeries to remove the valuable body parts. Their bodies are discarded like the carcasses of dead animals. In other trafficking venues, children are sold away for labor. Some work as domestic helpers. Others appear on the crowded city streets as professional beggars. Some are exploited for pornography. They may be sold to brothels, lodges, and hotels.

It is slavery. Human rights organizations have given clear definition.

The call for an end to human trafficking has been made. But the criminal, highly profitable enterprise goes on, mostly unchecked. Unchallenged.

Real change requires a willingness to enforce law and prosecute violators. It takes considerable resources. As Dr. Anantha took our film crew through the mean streets, he talked about the drug lords and mafia dons and foreigners with pockets filled with cash who control the streets. Interference with their flourishing business is high risk. It is a violent, shadowy underworld.

WHEN HEARTS CHANGE . . .

In his presentation, Dr. Anantha pointed to the causes of this inhuman, cruel menace. The top of most any list is poverty. The absence of adequate shelter, good nutrition, clean water, proper sanitation, basic preventative health care, adequate income, and proper clothing all contribute to a deep level of despair.

When opportunities for gainful employment are absent, when organized crime rules the streets and neighborhoods, when violence against women is an accepted norm, where the caste system prevents any possibility of crossover or upward mobility, where illiteracy reigns and education is out of reach, where the government is corrupt and weapons become the primary means of brute control, hope is gone.

> This is God's work. These forgotten, discarded people ache for a future to believe in.

As a committed Christian, Dr. Anantha takes it a step further. His perspective goes beyond the usual purview of academic, scholarly analysis. He simply states that what needs changing is the human heart. Lost people are hungry for a message of hope. They need the power of redemption. This is God's work. These forgotten, discarded people ache for a future to believe in.

When that spirit is awakened in the heart, then education becomes meaningful, purposeful, and effective.

Our team took notes as Anantha spoke at the whiteboard. They wanted not only to capture the compelling images they had seen on their amazing journey following Caden's cinematic tracks, but they also wanted to capture something of Anantha's compelling declaration that the heart can be changed.

The heart must be changed. The heart of the Dalit. The heart of the politician. The heart of the businessperson and the doctor, the educator and the farmer. The man in queue at the brothel's door. The artist. The musician.

As hearts change, the backbone of the caste system will be broken. Forever.

BACK HOME: ALL SIGNS GO

As Brent and Jon continued their preparation for the feature film, the plans back home for our Global Freedom initiative quickened. It was spring 2008. My motivation to lead had never been more intense. We pulled in a consulting firm. During this time, the economy continued to soar. The stock market reached new highs, real estate values continued to rise, and businesses posted record-breaking results. All the signs pointed to a successful campaign to take our plans forward both on a local and a global level.

We hired a consulting firm to help us lock in our strategy. We communicated our intentions with every tool at our disposal. We had open meetings. We took an online survey. I had individual conversations with potential major donors. We created a series of videos with an animated flyover of a computer-generated model of our expansion plans. We set our sights on twenty-three million dollars over three years.

I looked back on my own journey. I reflected on our near-century-old history as a church. I remembered the Marshburns, a significant founding family, and their commitment to building a successful business enterprise that would fund a kingdom initiative right here in Orange County. They were determined to impact the world in the name of Jesus. I thought about the years of sacrifice and visionary leadership. Then I thought about the near-tragedy, when midway into our building project in 2003, stresses and strains reached fever pitch, and we nearly lost everything we had worked to build. The church split wide open.

Now, in a few short years, everything had changed. All signs were "Go." The lights were green. Yes, there were some who feared what they called "donor fatigue." Some were not at all reticent about informing me that they believed our plans were more a product of my inflated ego than God's direction. I must tell you, that criticism stung. I remembered those dark days just after I left the church. I made a commitment: I would seek after God. It would not be self-promotion. Instead, I would seek Him first, and then I would stand for Him.

But I did not allow it to distract me from my primary role—to articulate a God-sized vision in a way that our people would see it, feel it, and mobilize around it. I was not alone. People smarter and more capable than I surrounded me. They saw it, too.

> Some informed me that
> they believed our plans
> were more a product of my
> inflated ego than God's
> direction. I must tell you,
> that criticism stung.

The results of our surveys were compiled. The data confirmed what we observed in the public meetings and the private conversations with donors large and small. Our lay leaders and staff affirmed the plan. It all bolstered my confidence that God was in it.

People are quick to tell you that I am a young pastor. Perhaps they have it right. But as I reflected on the journey, it felt like several lifetimes wrapped up into one. I thought back on the days when I recorded music as a college student, obsessed with the desire to make music.

When I was asked to be worship leader for a progressive church with a vision for growth, I accepted the role with all the enthusiasm that drove my passion for music. It was more than performance for me. I understood the music's power to shape lives, to change hearts, to challenge old prejudices, and bring a diverse people together in celebration and meaningful collaboration. I knew music had the power to draw people into the very presence of God.

As my responsibilities broadened in a growing congregation, my convictions about leadership deepened. My role would expand as a facilitator and visionary. I could see talent, sometime more than the person possessing that talent could. I would sketch out the possibilities and then step back and watch the blossom unfold. When we outgrew our original chapel and built a temporary structure to house the growing congregation, we designed it to maximize the impact of our weekend services. Finally, when we developed the master plan for the new worship center, it seemed as though nothing could stop us.

> In retrospect, I know now that I was part of the problem.

But something did—as we have already seen.

I reflected on the day I was told I no longer had a place on the team. The clashing agendas, the backroom debates, the pressures of this scale of development were just too much. In retrospect, I know now that I was part of the problem. My enthusiasms got the best of me. Those were hard days.

Out of my disorientation and those periods of introspection came the vision for The River. It was a confirmation of my gifts. It reinforced the notion that I really do believe in the church. I have strong ideas about method and strategy. But when Jesus commissioned the church to represent Him in the world, He meant it. Throughout history, the church has logged too many misfires. But in spite of the abuses on record and rehearsed by some as a convenient excuse to avoid God, He has always had His faithful remnant. The church has powerfully promoted God's purpose and reflected His heart throughout history. I considered other career paths, but none had enough appeal to pull me away from my passion for the church—and the power of the church to proclaim the Gospel that transforms lives and society and culture and even history. The River taught me that.

I remembered those deeply emotional meetings with the elders when we confessed our shortcomings and misgivings and misunderstandings and our selfish ambitions. God brought us together in the most powerful reconciliation I have ever witnessed. It brought healing and restored hope. It launched a new era of vision and growth. The humility and compassion of those individuals at that critical moment is a memory I will cherish for the rest of my life.

The hunt for vision began. It was always more than a building project for me. I did not know at the time that I would find that vision half a world away. I thought about my arrival at Hyderabad's old airport and my first impressions of India and the meeting with D'souza and the visits to Pipe Village and Uddamarri School and that night at the Corporate Stay Hotel that forever changed me. "I'm in," I told God. "I am so in."

Brent and I high-fived each other when we came up with the concept of Global Freedom in the pool in New Delhi. It was a God moment. And then I contemplated all the amazing things that unfolded after that day—how all of our people connected with the plight of the Dalit people. It was as though there is something of the Dalit in us all. When we witness the power of the Gospel to free a Dalit from a life of despair to a vision of meaning and purpose and wholeness, it impacts all of us. We all are desperate for that same liberating power. And it is available to us all.

Global Freedom energized all of our initiatives. We were poised for the launch. All systems GO.

Word spread. People began to call, asking how we did it. I got invitations to speak.

We set the calendar for the fall. We printed the materials. We produced the DVD for the documentary short, *Delete*. We built a website. We created the database. We trained our small group leaders. We wrote curriculum for our children and our students. We held a series of open meetings. We designed our teaching schedule and coordinated the themes with our worship and arts team.

All of our plans were in place.

AND THEN . . .

I had been attending a weeklong conference in Denver. After the last conference session that week, I returned to my hotel eager to get a good night's sleep before my early morning return flight to Orange County the next day. At three o'clock in the morning, I was awakened from a deep sleep. I don't know why. I rolled over and noticed a text message on my BlackBerry. "Conference call at 7AM. Important." That is all it said. The sender was my close friend and our head elder. I knew it would not be good. That was the last of my sleep.

I got myself together and dialed in promptly four hours later.

As I listened to the voices on the other end of the phone, the news hit me hard. My heart sank in my chest. A short time later, as I boarded an airplane in Denver, on my way home, a great sadness overwhelmed me.

A key staff pastor, one of my closest friends, was in crisis. It was personal. The details don't belong in a book.

Just know this: it was a crushing blow. It went to the heart of everything we had worked toward together. I met face-to-face with my colleague and fellow staff pastor and friend. One-on-one. We looked hard at the truth. We wept.

At that crucial moment, we were once more put to the test.

Too many churches, in the name of righteousness, destroy the person in order to save him. I asked God for the wisdom of Solomon. The compassion of Jesus. The insight of Paul. The winsome, easy camaraderie of Peter. I called in our best and our brightest. We knew we were, all of us, facing our Enemy.

I had a laundry list of questions. I wrote them all down. There was a lot I did not know. But one thing I did know. It was an unavoidable conclusion.

In spite of all our meticulous planning, the high-octane churchwide anticipation, and the gaping need on the other side of the world; even though all that was in place and ready for launch, we all agreed.

Global Freedom must wait.

Chapter 10

WAITING

MARDI OFTEN CHALLENGES ME with the stuff she is reading. She is a great resource. Late in the summer of 2008, she picked up *Fasting*, by Jentezen Franklin. She passed it along. We had a long talk about what she learned.

Before that, neither of us paid much attention to this biblical discipline. It was never a focus of either of our church traditions. We knew there were many who found it meaningful. We had studied enough Bible on our own to know that fasting has a place in spiritual development. We simply wanted to know more.

It is a curious "coincidence." Our talks centered on fasting at the very time when this unexpected crisis blindsided us. When the news came regarding my fellow staff pastor, our world froze.

Global Freedom went on hold.

Our devotional book taught us some timely lessons. Fasting is a way to interrupt our routines; to learn what it feels like to sacrifice. Most important, fasting positions us to listen. It requires intentionality. So much of our prayer life involves addressing God. We speak to God about our concerns, about the obstacles that hold us back, about relationships in turmoil, about demands that will not let up, about our confusion. But in our talks, Mardi and I recognized our need to learn more about what it means to be still, to be in a heightened state of alert. That is a tough assignment in our high-intensity world, not to mention a houseful of growing children.

It went against all my instincts to put our Global Freedom campaign aside. We had overcome so many barriers. There were so many confirmations. So much was at stake. We were on the right track. I fully believed that. There were many excuses we could have grabbed hold of to let it go. Some would have been relieved if we had.

But now we faced something that required us to stop. To reflect . . . to consider . . . to listen. To wait.

To wait on God.

LEARNING TO BE A WAITER

Biblically, waiting on God is not the same as waiting for someone who has been delayed, as in holding up dinner until guests arrive after battling an unexpected traffic jam. Waiting on God is more like a server waiting tables. The server listens, records each order, pays special attention to detail, and then personally delivers each carefully prepared entrée one at a time. The good ones understand the power of presentation—placement, order, timing. Back in the day, they were not called servers but waiters. Waiting on God, then, is not just finding a way to mark time. It is, rather, listening to God's desires, getting a sense of His preferences, the things that meet His needs. What it is that will please and bring joy.

Fasting while waiting was a new concept for Mardi and me. We tried it. We skipped a meal here and there. We were complete novices.

In time, I came to realize that I had been learning to wait on God all along. The fasting helped me see it. Waiting on God energized my passion for Dalit freedom. In visiting the Dalits and listening to them, I was, in a powerful way, waiting on God's table. My efforts to get the word out and mobilize people and resources to meet the needs I found was like serving God in the way a master chef prepares cuisine in a fine restaurant.

This illustration has appeared in my sermons before. I have imagined Jesus coming to my house for dinner. What would we serve? How would we prepare? I have asked our people to imagine the same. What would they do?

Mardi and I developed an appetite for this kind of relationship with God. These insights flooded our hearts and our conversations on those days when we intentionally missed a meal and instead, found a quiet place to reflect and open ourselves to the living presence of the living God. We would feel the hunger pangs. And we would think about our brothers and sisters in India, Dalits, young and old, especially those in the slums who feel those pangs on a regular basis. In those moments of increased focus and heightened sensitivities, we were that much closer.

> When I announced that Global Freedom would be postponed, there was an audible gasp.

I know full well that Jesus warned us not to talk about these things publicly. But as strongly as I felt the need to put this herculean task of Global Freedom on hold, I felt just as strongly that our people, all of us, needed to take time to listen. To hear God speak. To prepare ourselves for spiritual service; to get ourselves ready for spiritual opposition. To strengthen our walk. To depend less on ourselves and more on Him.

So I scrubbed the Global Freedom series. Our leadership team concurred. We eliminated the original plan for our fall weekend worship service and turned our attention instead to the biblical topic of fasting and prayer.

When I announced that Global Freedom would be postponed, there was an audible gasp. For those who wanted a fuller explanation, we would have open meetings. Several hundred people attended. In every case, there was full support. People understood. We needed to focus on caring for our staff. And we did. God is working in a powerful way to bring forgiveness, reconciliation, and hope.

But I also announced my conviction, shared by our leadership, that it was time to turn our attention to God. It was time for some healthy introspection. I knew that if we were going to move forward toward Global Freedom, we needed to be open before God, to let Him do His work in us as a collection of individuals. There seemed to be no better way than to consider the biblical discipline of fasting. We spent several weekends exploring the teaching of Jesus and Paul. We looked at the Old Testament, too. We provided materials with tips on fasting. Be wise. Talk to your doctor. We made it clear: this is no legalistic requirement. This is not a way to pile up merit badges for entry into heaven. Each individual will determine in his or her own heart what the right response might be to this teaching. We laid out many potential options.

A spirit of humility and openness moved over our people. It was as though I could see the pettiness and the complaints and the cynicism that so easily accompany new initiatives just melt away. In those services, our hearts were softened. Instead of informing God of our needs, as though He did not know them, we simply listened. We waited on God, each in our own way. There was a sweetness about it that remains with me to this day.

I had no way of knowing why we were moved in this direction. But I would soon learn.

A BUBBLE BURSTS

Our goals for Global Freedom were set as the economy surged. While we made our plans, our capitalist system fueled growth everywhere. I am no expert, but I knew that China's economy was charging forward. There were signs of spectacular growth in the technology sector in India. All over the world, as Thomas Friedman pointed out, thanks to Internet connectivity and an unprecedented point-to-point delivery system, access to markets moved forward at an unprecedented pace.

But by the time we called off our plans to launch Global Freedom and we determined to wait in open anticipation of hearing God's voice, concerns about the economy had escalated.

As we approached the autumn of 2008, market fears stirred. Some noted that the white-hot growth of the global economy could not go on indefinitely. I did not give it much thought. Markets go in cycles. I knew that much from the lower division courses I took back in my undergraduate days. Smart people always seemed to figure it out. There are always those prophets of doom who predict the worst. I did not pay it much attention during the summer of 2008.

But then came September 2008, a month that will forever remain prominent in the unfolding history of the global economy.

US housing values had reached impossibly high levels. Easy credit drove the expansion of new neighborhoods all over the country. New cars filled many of those garages, many of them financed by new loans on residences with ever-increasing value. In our world, it seemed that the entire advertising industry focused on mortgage loans. "Get your hands on the cash waiting in the equity of your house," the radio blared. Every day. Everyone remodeled, it seemed. Upgrades everywhere. It did not require a master's degree to know that something had to give. And in September 2008, it did.

During the year, those housing values leveled off and then began to drop. Sales of new homes slowed. Across the country, loan balances exceeded home values. The foreclosure debacle was about to begin.

The headlines announced that the two largest federal mortgage companies would be taken over by a receiver. We now know that the system was about to purge itself. It would not be pretty. The government's admission that the two enormous federal lending institutions were on the verge of collapse sent an alarming message to the financial world.

On September 28, 2008, the market responded to the bad news. It triggered the largest point drop in stock market history. Reality set in. The market had lost nearly one-third of its value since October the prior year. Trillions of dollars in value vanished in twelve short months. The nation seemed helpless as congressional leaders met with financial giants, and the federal government moved quickly to stop the hemorrhaging.

I stood before a congregation who sat quietly in our new worship center in a palpable state of shock.

Just one year before, the newspaper had called our church's community the wealthiest neighborhood in America. But on the following Sunday morning, I stood before a congregation who sat quietly in our new worship center in a palpable state of shock. Knowing it was a delicate subject, one of our staff pastors said on that Sunday morning, "Well, we've all looked at the value of our retirement accounts this week, haven't we?" Silence.

Then he continued, "We're learning that our confidence does not come from the Dow Jones Industrial Average, aren't we?" He smiled as a muted, nervous laughter followed. We all knew the truth he pointed us toward. Sometimes we learn it best when the anxiety is high.

For the entire month, and following, we digested the headlines. Major financial institutions whose logos inspired trust and confidence and bullishness toward our nation's fundamental strength were now on the brink of collapse. There were mergers, and bankruptcy filings, bailouts, partisan wrangling, and all-out efforts to prevent a general panic. Talk of unemployment, loss of consumer confidence, the rippling effect, the international currency implications, all of it dominated the headlines in all forms of media as back home we sorted through the Scriptures and fasted and prayed.

Just a few months earlier, I knew that we needed to take time to listen. I wanted our people to hear God's "still small voice." But I did not expect Him to pull out (to borrow a familiar metaphor from C. S. Lewis) a megaphone. In an astounding, supernatural way, our time of fasting and prayer prepared us as a body of believers for this moment in ways I never could have. As we digested this turn of events, it became abundantly clear. Had we launched on our planned schedule, our appeal would have been made simultaneous to the greatest financial crisis our nation had faced since the Great Depression. But instead of pushing forward against impossible circumstances, we were poised to hear God's voice. Each of us needed a custom-made message. And that is exactly what God gave us.

Many needed to reassess. The comfort or perceived security that came from homeowner equity and burgeoning retirement accounts and investment portfolios was directly challenged. The mistaken notion that we could simply ride the wave of apparent success *en perpetuity* was exposed for the fraud that it is. We were brought face-to-face with the reality that wealth is fleeting. The pride that comes from excess is dangerous—and short-lived. It brought us back to biblical truth. And in the fear that surrounded us, we found water in the well. God made Himself real. We drew on His fresh supply.

And because we were listening, we found a peace that passes understanding even as the rest of the world appeared to be lost in turmoil.

But the unexpected struck again.

HILLS AFIRE

When you enter our pleasant town, a sign welcomes you to "The Land of Gracious Living." Years ago, as the Los Angeles basin grew in population and global influence, people came to our village for the citrus groves, rolling hills, and wide-open vistas. They brought their horses and stables and created a network of trails that wander along the creek beds and eucalyptus trees. It was an escape from those high-rise urban offices and crowded intersections and asphalt parking lots.

But even the best of our town would be tested in the fall of 2008, as the winds of financial crisis blew with ominous force. And yet the financial crisis was not the only thing that struck us.

When I woke up on Saturday morning, November 15, 2008, the scent of smoke was in the air. I looked out my window and saw nothing. I shrugged it off as just another Southern California day. By midmorning, my cell rang. I picked up. A fire rode the wind though the Green River Canyon, headed directly toward a residential area where several of our families lived. I turned on the local television station. Helicopters caught the scene.

> Mardi and I watched and listened. We thought about what we would rush to pack in a last-minute evacuation.

The raging brushfire headed directly toward Yorba Linda.

Every year, we live with fire season here in Southern California. The lack of rainfall combined with long dry summers means that by September and October, open spaces all across our vast counties are filled with the tinder of dry brush. All it takes is a spark. Anywhere. A small ignition will quickly burst into gluttonous flames that create their own winds. Hot oxygen becomes explosive fuel for expanding fires. Glowing hot embers may go airborne, riding the wind, igniting everything along the way. As the heat intensifies in the abundance of fuel, trees turn to giant blowtorches. If there is a residence in the path of this reign of terror, its rooftop is vulnerable, and an entire structure can be lost in a matter of minutes.

If the winds came our way, our own home would have been threatened. Mardi and I watched and listened. We thought about what we would rush to pack in a last-minute evacuation. Neighborhoods were quickly blocked off as our town attracted firefighting units from all over the county. Soon there were aerial drops of water and chemicals, but the flames continued on across the ridge all the way over to the next town. We could see homes going up in flames.

Our church received calls all morning from our people. We set up a help center, opening our doors for evacuees coming down from the hills. We learned that on the edges of the neighborhoods, homes were under siege. At the higher altitudes up the hill, even in our planned upscale communities, water pressure gave out. Estate homes along the ridge were exposed, unprotected.

By one o'clock that Saturday afternoon, more than twenty homes in our town alone were gone. Helicopters brought the terrifying video images of burning houses to our television screens in high definition. I considered the plight of these folks who had planted themselves in "the land of gracious living" who woke up that morning as I did, perhaps catching the faint smell of smoke in the air, who now were left with nothing but a smoldering slab of concrete, a blackened chimney, twisted metal, and everything they owned destroyed—gone up in smoke.

When the flames were finally brought under control two days later, nearly two hundred homes were completely destroyed. Another 130 were severely damaged. Many more homeowners suffered from the lingering blanket of smoke and ash. Meanwhile, swimming pools filled with gray mush, cinder, and charred branches, and landscaping blackened beyond recognition. The intense heat took its toll: white polyurethane fences melted like wax; wrought-iron gates twisted and turned. Many of us had assumed that our protected neighborhoods were invincible. As we surveyed the devastation, we came to understand. Our lives and everything we think we own are but a vapor.

YOU SHALL NOT BE BURNED . . .

The weekend of the fires was our lowest attendance for worship in more than a decade. We considered canceling services. But many expressed the need to be together. To worship. To pray for the victims of our hometown fires. To enter into the presence of the living God. In the months that brought us to this moment in time, we had come face-to-face with the tragic plight of Dalits on the other side of the globe. That Saturday morning, we knew something of the devastating and indiscriminate and destructive power of forces beyond our control; the fire's appetite can take a home and lives in minutes. It leaves an unimaginable disorder in its wake.

Because we were listening, lessons were learned; truth embraced. There were prayer meetings on burned sites. Camera crews picked up the scenes of believers huddled together, hands on shoulders, tears flowing, calling on a living God. They broadcasted those scenes unedited on the nationwide feed. Church members delivered cash cards for Home Depot, local restaurants, and grocery stores. We assembled a group of professionals to assist homeowners with insurance issues and utility challenges, to assist in negotiating with government agencies, and to help folks in shock find temporary housing, clothing, and food.

Believers reached out to run errands, provide rides, bring assistance, and embrace families devastated by the fires. One of our members owns an upscale restaurant on the top of a prominent hill the next town over. We worked together to host a first-rate banquet for firefighters, community leaders, and those who suffered loss to share a meal and just listen to their stories over fine food.

As things settled down, in the aftermath of the fire, I sat down with our teaching team to reflect. We all noticed the same thing. I brought a copy of the sermon notes I had prepared for the weekend of the terrible firestorm that swept through our town. The name of the series we had chosen the summer before had an eerie effect on us all.

Right there on the top of the page was the unlikely title: *"Send the Fire!"* We shook our heads in disbelief. Then we changed the title.

The morning following the Yorba Linda fire, I talked about Isaiah 43:2–3 (NKJV): "When you pass through the waters, I will be with you; and through the rivers, they shall not overflow you. When you walk through the fire, you shall not be burned, nor shall the flame scorch you. For I am the Lord your God." Isaiah's words brought comfort to us all.

GOD'S PAUSE, GOD'S PROTECTION

Just four months before, we had been moving with complete confidence toward the launch of our Global Freedom campaign. But unanticipated circumstances brought it all to a temporary halt. We were tempted to ask "why?"

At the time, we didn't know the answer to that question. But two months into our time of listening, fasting, and prayer, we understood something powerful about God's grand design. God put us on pause for a purpose. He used the most unlikely circumstances. Before we launched a global initiative, He needed to teach us something poignant about purity and wholeness, forgiveness and reconciliation. Service. Availability. Openness. He prepared us for an unprecedented period of national calamity. He wanted us to be ready to respond to crisis in our own backyard.

And during those autumn months, we learned something powerful about waiting on God. He taught us about the needs in our own house and our own neighborhood that prepared us to reach out halfway around the world.

Sometimes I sit and wonder what may have happened if we had not paused. We would not have given the time necessary to care properly for a staff pastor in crisis. We would have asked for financial commitments at the same time Congress was reluctantly approving a near-trillion-dollar bailout to prop up a failing economy against complete and total collapse. We would have been reeling from a weakened campaign, devastated by a dramatic decline of market values, the evaporation of credit, and the near-standstill of business activity as those fires came over the ridge attacking our town with a vengeance.

All that on what was to be Commitment Sunday.

But God, in His wisdom and grace, protected us.

Now, at year's end, we were faced with new questions: Do we press on, or do we retreat? Do we conform to a national psychology of gloom and fear? Do we acquiesce to those who considered the calamities of recent months to be a sign, a signal that we should shut down our plan to reach out to those Dalit people on the other side of the globe?

Or do we trust God on a whole new level, believing that what He started He will enable all the way to the finish?

I remembered my hero, Joshua. I do not know that I can convey in words the depth of transformation that gripped me back on that night at the Corporate Stay Hotel. I could not for a moment imagine an abandonment of those children, those people.

> The lessons learned prepared us to offer a commitment that would be truly transformational.

God customizes the impact of any given event for each individual. I believe that. A rainstorm can be a blessing for some, an annoyance for others. Same storm, different effect. It is beyond my capacity to comprehend. But I hold on to that faith. The global economic tide that advances and then retreats impacts us all in various ways. A blazing out-of-control fire moves with the winds. It all may seem random, and yet it is not. I look for God in both success and failure. As Job said, "The Lord gave, and the Lord has taken away; blessed be the name of the Lord" (1:21 NKJV).

But nothing in me considered the surprises of the past few months to be cause to jettison our pledge to the children of the slums of India. On the contrary, I believed that the lessons learned prepared us, in ways we had not been prepared, to offer a commitment that would be truly transformational.

Up until September 2008, we trusted our investment portfolios to fund our campaign. We believed our successful businesses would carry us through. Up until that fateful day when the scent of burning brush filled the air and billows of smoke clouded the morning sun, we trusted the security and value of our real estate to position us to help. Too many of us were lax in our attitudes toward personal purity and faithfulness to our commitments. God, in His own way, addressed all of those issues in a powerful way, while we waited. And fasted. And prayed.

A new conviction got hold of me. I had spoken the words before. But now, the reality of those words gripped me somewhere deeper than I had ever known. We will trust God for the resources. We will believe in His promise. "I will never leave you nor forsake you." God said it clearly to Joshua.[1]

This was no time to abandon the children lost in caste, untouchable, caught in persecution and abuse, the young victims of the thugs who would rather trade the beautiful children for a profit than empower them for a life of independence and purpose. This is no time to abandon the slum families, the mothers separated from their offspring and fathers unable to provide.

Nor could we forsake those who needed us closer to home.

Our leaders met. They were aware of the concerns of some on the periphery. But none favored withdrawal. Not one. Our staff felt the same. A burning conviction smoldered somewhere inside; with reckless abandon, we would trust God. This was not the irresponsible course. It was the most responsible thing we could possibly do.

There were tears. There were confessions of utter dependence on the God who created us in His image, who redeemed us through the eternal work of His Son, who energized us to be His representatives in a broken and needy world. Those prayer times were unforgettable.

I spoke to our major donors. The market drop had adversely impacted nearly all of them. Some had to reduce their commitment by a fraction. But all of them said yes, and stood by their prior commitment. They told me not simply that we ought to move forward but that we *must* move forward. God had shown His faithfulness in so many ways, it would be a tragic misread to doubt Him now.

So as we gathered after celebrating Christmas and a New Year, we announced it: Global Freedom would proceed. With God's help, we would move forward into an uncertain future with confidence, not in ourselves but in Him.

So, as we launched the New Year 2009, we picked up right where we left off that day several months earlier when I got that text message before

boarding a flight home from Denver to Orange County. I reflected over
and over again on the amazing things that happened since that day. A staff
pastor. A global economic crisis. A devastating fire. Prayer and fasting.
Renewal. Restoration. Reconciliation. Redemption. Humility. Tears.
Laughter. Contentment. Joy. Anticipation.

All this as we crossed our personal Jordan River entering our Promised Land. We had not arrived, but we were discovering a powerful God
who gives us a vision of what can be, and what will be, and then enables us
to bring something of the coming kingdom to the here and now.

We know that the battle is not over. We know that there will be more
distractions and surprises when the unexpected and the unplanned interrupt us. But we are better prepared now. The fasting and the prayers
will continue. We picked up those materials and charts and plans, and
we rewrote the calendar. Under the banner of Global Freedom, we would
make a substantial giant step toward the mission ahead.

Jesus told His followers to go out into all the world and to make disciples. That is the essence of Global Freedom. Here at home. The next town
over. And on the other side of the world.

I tried my best to communicate that vision, with every verbal resource
I could pull together. Three words sum it up: *extend, expand,* and *enlarge.*
Our intent is simply to extend our lives, to expand our influence, and
enlarge our impact. Jesus challenged people to look inward and exam-
ine their hearts. But there was always a purpose in that introspection.
Healthy self-analysis leads to service and outreach. I came back to my
starting place as a pastor. Our focus should not be inward but outward.
As we reach out with a message of hope, others find the liberating power
of the Gospel. And as others are changed, so are we. That is the message
of Global Freedom.

Aaron Blanton, our worship leader, was prompted by the vision of
Global Freedom to write a song. It has been produced as a music video.
I am convinced that the images and words and phrases will impact the

whole world. His lyric captures the essence of our initiative. It is high inspiration. It is a powerful challenge. The title is "We Are the Hands."

> *We still debate the second coming of Christ*
> *While half of the world hasn't heard of the first.*
> *How can we wait or just close our eyes*
> *While half of the world is dying of thirst?*
>
> *Let's swing the doors wide open*
> *And hammer down dividing walls*
>
> > *We are the hands*
> > *We are the feet*
> > *We are the voice of love for the least of these*
> > *We are the hands*
> > *We are the feet*
> > *Love is a language the whole world speaks*
> > *We are the hands.*
>
> *We still debate what style of worship we'll bring*
> *While half of the world has no reason to sing.*
> *The heart of God is with the poor and oppressed*
> *Why should we wait and call ourselves "blessed"? . . .*
> *What if I? What if you . . .*
>
> > *Give up what we cannot keep*
> > *To gain what we cannot lose?*
> > *What will last? What will stand?*
> > *What will matter in the end?*
>
> *Only love.*
> *We are the hands.*[2]

Aaron captured Jesus' challenge. We become Jesus to those who have
no options. As we prepared for our launch Sunday, we anticipated the de-
but of the music video. All our inside planners watched and listened. "We

Are the Hands" became our theme song as we worked toward the biggest Sunday in our history.

The timing of all this became synchronized with God's clock, not ours. With a new, improved timetable, a historic, groundbreaking event in India coincided with our new launch date. We reintroduced all our materials. We prepared presentations for folks we knew would be on the front lines with us. We compiled the stories of God's amazing work among us.

But best of all, perfect timing, I got on an airplane for India with a handful of our leaders, on our way to the first-ever high school graduation of Dalit children. I would meet with Dr. D'souza again in his office with my friends and colleagues there in Central India just two weeks before launch Sunday back home. What a reunion it would be.

Notes

1. Joshua 1:5.
2. "We Are the Hands," ©2008 by Aaron Blanton. Used by permission.

Chapter 11

COMMENCEMENT

THE LUXURY OF THE NEW Airbus 380 jet felt like a sharp contrast to the purpose of my trip. The amenities and the appointments and the accessibility of entertainment options and creature comforts on this first leg of our journey back to India were a welcome sight as we boarded the aircraft for a sixteen-hour nonstop flight from Los Angeles to Dubai.

Traveling with me was a collection of good friends, several of whom had sacrificed significantly for Global Freedom's cause. Perhaps the most unlikely traveler on our team was Jorge Norena, lead pastor of the growing Hispanic branch of our church. Every Sunday, Jorge preaches to an expanding crowd in Spanish. To my amazement, he caught the vision of providing Dalit children with an English education. In an outpouring of love and support, his whole church has committed to supporting the construction of Dalit schools. *"¡Libertad Global!"* they shouted in unison.

OVER THE OCEAN, LOOKING BACK

We settled in for a long flight. I pulled out my iPod and headset, fired up some worship music, and sat there with my eyes closed. We were two weeks away from our official launch of Global Freedom. On our way to witness the first high school graduation of the Dalit Education Centers, I did not quite know what to expect. And I was physically spent.

I reflected on the Christmas season. Attendance was over 30 percent higher than the previous year. Over seven thousand people from our community joined us on Christmas Eve for a timely celebration of the birth of Jesus, the one who inspired and sustained the whole Global Freedom movement worldwide. Our people got a taste of it. Our worship and arts team pulled off a memorable night of drama and music. Families streamed into multiple services to witness the power of music and the timeless Scriptures that speak of God's presence and grace in the incarnation. God became flesh.

On the first Sunday of the New Year, we had given our annual "state of the church" address. It is a long-standing tradition for me to review the highlights of the prior year and to paint the picture of the vision for the year to come. That weekend, I rehearsed the long history of our church, looking toward our 2012 centennial celebration. As I spoke, I saw the faces of those who had stood with us as I returned to the staff midcrisis. I asked them to join me in completing the task we started together.

My noise-canceling headset blocked out the roar of the four giant engines. The worship set put me in a pensive mood. It got me thinking about the greatness of God. His indescribable goodness, His incomprehensible ways. It was the end of February. Mid-March, we would launch. I pulled my journal out of my briefcase. I leafed through the pages and reread a few entries from the beginning of the year.

January 5, 2009

Well this weekend I presented our vision in all three services! It was awesome— God showed up and moved!! I can't believe I get to be a part of this!!

John 10:27 "My sheep hear my voice and I know them. They hear my voice and follow me."

God, that is my prayer for our church and for me. Pretty awesome to think the God of the universe knows me. To experience Christmas Eve with over seven thousand people. To watch you move with so many visitors. You showed up and blessed. To look at Sunday's attendance and see more people, more babies, more excitement. I love your church and I love serving in this place.

Thank you, God.

All of those difficult nights and days. All of those prayer meetings. All of the planning. All of the counsel. The tragedies emerged to teach us— not about God's abandonment and cruelty, but about His care and grace and faithfulness. And then I turned the page.

January 9, 2009

Today I got to meet with three large donors. I spent the day gathering wise counsel, seeking your wisdom through others. Today was good. All of them were amazingly supportive. All of them said the same thing: move forward now.

God, thank you for faithful people.

Tomorrow I continue the process. I can't wait to see what you do. A movie? Are you kidding me? Wow, God you are so much bigger than me and my thinking.

You have flat blown us away with the strategic connections and the wide open door of opportunity.

May we be faithful.

Keep us from greed, consumption, pride.

Keep us from doing this for the wrong reasons.

God–help us stay pure.

I stopped reading and contemplated for a while. It is a powerful thing to put your thoughts in writing. So often, those written words become prophetic; almost as though the writing provides a link between past and present and future. I turned the page. It hit me hard. My journal entries are really prayers.

January 15, 2009

"Open your mouth for the speechless, in the cause of all who are appointed to die. Open your mouth, judge righteously, and plead the cause of the poor and needy." Proverbs 31:8–9

I spent the day with Dr. D'souza, sharing the vision and moving forward your kingdom!

We presented the movie "Open Wide Your Hearts" which sounds a little too much like church, but has a great message. He was stoked. Aaron's song can become the theme of the whole movement.

God can do the immeasurable, more than we could think or imagine!

God—this movie thing is big. Can you [I know you can]; will you provide? Please Lord; I am out on a limb here. Help me get it right for you and your kingdom. This is a huge project; a lot of money. But I believe the time is now!

Continue to show me what I cannot see. I need that today, and I want that for our future. Bless Brent and Jon with your story. Give them your words and your mind as they write, dear God. God, we are making a difference. Please protect us. Guide us. Show us. Help us. And Father, move us toward you and your heart.

Global Freedom—God I am stepping out here. Will you please not let me fall too far? I know I need whatever you have for me. So right now I give myself over to you for the movement—I am yours, oh God. Use me, enlarge my capacity to lead. Give me courage to ask for the big gifts. We need it!

May I cultivate a generous church by the leading of your spirit. May they see the needs of the lost and those far from you and may they give openly, happily, liberally!

Thank you for the call on our lives that is stretching, painful, time-consuming, and energizing. It has opened doors of opportunity like never before.

I closed the leather-bound journal and then closed my eyes. Emotion welled up in me somewhere between Iceland and Ireland, midway between Los Angeles and Dubai. My friends were asleep. The cabin was dark, except for a few reading lamps like mine. Several monitors flickered here and there in the darkness, all tuned to some personal movie selection. Everyone had his or her own audio. But there I was, far from home, bound for a place even farther, clear and clean worship music filling my ears and my heart. The captivating sense of God's presence filled me up. The emotion turned to rest; a kind of rare contentment that comes by sweet surprise.

And then I slipped into a deep, satisfying sleep.

THE SCHOOL GOD BUILT

The next day, I was in the same office in the heart of India as the year before. Here, Dr. D'souza had made an impassioned plea for Dalit schools. I was taken then by his cogent argument, and now, I am amazed by what has happened since. He laid out the case. He set the bar high: *one thousand schools.* The goal is nothing less than the elimination of the caste system in all of India, and thus, the world. He envisioned the end of slavery. It triggered something in me that to this day I cannot fully explain. That was the day I said it out loud: "I am committed to finding the resources to build two hundred of those one thousand schools."

And now, I am back in that same office again, with my good friend and partner in ministry Joseph D'souza. This time, we are preparing for a milestone moment in the movement, the first-ever graduation of Dalits who have completed an English education from three of our schools. We are not really prepared for the power of the event. That will come after two eventful days.

D'souza's staff takes good care of us. Our team ate heartily. Fragrant basmati rice and colorful vegetables, fresh fruits, coconut, curry, lentils, lamb, chicken, fried potatoes, and paneer cheese.

Our new partnership made us comfortable with each other now. There was mutual trust, easy conversation. I encouraged our team to ask questions. It was a lively discussion. Joseph spoke freely about the early days, about his life partner, Mariam, and their children. He talked about his friendship with Udit Raj and how together they birthed a passion for Dalit freedom. He spoke with pride about his daughter, Beryl, who took after her mother. She was a keen student, bright, witty, curious. She excelled in all her classes. The day came when she was accepted into medical school. Her dreams of a career in medicine came true when she completed her formal class work, her residency, and then passed her board exams. I like to call Beryl "the real Dr. D'souza."

> The sound of the children in the playground fills the air as a living soundtrack for a hope and a future.

We go for a tour of the grounds. Over the past quarter century, the campus had grown. But something very special had happened in the two years since my first visit. We had joined others in making a substantial investment in the expansion of the elementary school right there in Hyderabad. We monitored the progress, but now I turn the corner past a high thick hedge, and for the first time, I see it.

Three stories. "U" shaped. Over twenty classrooms. A large courtyard. Freshly painted. I stop in amazement. As I look from one end to the other, a stream of young uniformed students in a straight line files out the door and into the school grounds. They laugh and tease as children do, and one more time, the scene opens up and emotion grips me. I do not think the children could see it, but tears stream down my face. Our church, on the other side of the globe, helped make this happen. Their vision. Their gifts. Their prayers. Their sacrifice. Their love. All of it comes together. The sound of the children in the playground fills the air as a living soundtrack for a hope and a future.

But there is more to come.

THE GOOD SHEPHERD GRADUATION

The next morning we prepare for the graduation ceremony. Joseph approaches, his hand on my shoulder. "I would like very much for you to issue a challenge to our graduates, Matthew. You have been a tremendous encouragement to the whole team and me. Would you?"

"I would be honored," is all I can think to say.

That afternoon, as our team watches a two-hour video presentation on the caste system in India, I write my speech. I take a pen to a blank page. But before I write, I ask God to give me the words to say. It is closing in on me. This is a significant responsibility. This is a watershed day for these young, bright, talented teenagers. It is a defining moment for them. Without the vision of Dr. D'souza, it may have never been. And now I am in it, too. I have put my stake in the ground. I am invested. No turning back.

I put the finishing touches on my handwritten commencement speech. And as I consider my words and edit and refine, I reflect on what has been happening in our own family of believers back home. Many were praying for our small team sitting around that table watching that film at that very moment in time. Many were wishing they could be here with us; many whose hearts had been captured. Like mine.

Darkness falls as we walk into the open courtyard of the brand-new three-story elementary school, the hallowed ground where graduates will gather for an historic milestone. They have worked hard. They are surrounded by support. They have approached learning with unbridled enthusiasm. They have tasted the sweet rewards of diligence and persistence. They are hooked on discovery. They have uncovered their potential for intellectual and spiritual growth. Hopelessness has been supplanted by an eager anticipation of a new world of possibilities.

A banner hangs from the top floor of the new building and announces GOOD SHEPHERD HIGH SCHOOL. I know the Good Shepherd. Rows of seats for well over a thousand people are in place. The hard bare ground is covered. A stage is at the front with a black backdrop and colorful triangular shapes making it come alive under the bright lights. Video cameras surround the stage to capture every moment. Up-tempo music sets the mood through a speaker system that would accommodate a rock concert.

Parents, grandparents, dignitaries all file in. We are welcomed as esteemed visitors, brightly colored, ribboned welcome badges identifying us as honored guests. Dr. D'souza arrives with his lovely wife, Mariam. He is dressed in a white high-collar jacket and starched white shirt. Mariam is in her sari, bright shades of festive blue sweeping across. Their badges are conspicuously in place, like ours. They appear every bit the royal couple on this night of nights. As soon as I see the two of them, I know this is the culmination of their life's work. It is what they poured themselves into with all their hearts; and now the day has arrived. It is a completion, but it is also the beginning of a new chapter in the saga of Dalit Freedom in India.

> We would not want to be anywhere else on planet Earth than right here on the far side of the globe for this miraculous moment in time.

I look down the row at my team. They are wide-eyed. They know it. They are so far from home, in such an unfamiliar place. But they understand. The significance of this moment is not wasted on them. I can see the transformation happening with just a glance. They will never again be the same.

Dr. D'souza takes to the microphone. Everyone is in place. The dignitaries have all arrived. "It is a great privilege for me to introduce to you," and his voice catches, emotion grabbing him by the throat, "the first graduating class of the Good Shepherd Schools, the Class of 2009!"

The music swells. And from the shadows, they appear. They enter the great outdoor hall, each in a bright blue cap and gown with a yellow tassel swooshing back and forth as they stride in single file. The massive crowd stands. The applause and the whistles and the cheers rise up from the great assembly, filling the night air. These young students, knowing something of the power of the moment, break into broad smiles and laughter with a sense of pride and identity that would have, without D'souza's vision, forever eluded them.

Emotion overtakes me again. I cannot stop it. Tears roll down my cheeks. I clap so hard my hands hurt. I check on my team down the row. They are macho, strong guys, yet we are all the same. Tearstained. We look each other in the eye, up and down the aisle and nod in approval as we applaud and the cheers and hoots and music deafen us. We do not need to say anything. We are all thinking the same thing. We would not want to be anywhere else on planet Earth than right here on the far side of the globe for this miraculous moment in time.

The program launches. There are orations by politicians, educators, and scholars. Colorful and lively dance routines. Visiting dignitaries bring words of greeting and congratulations. Top students make speeches. Special video presentations give a sense of perspective, history, and focus on the accomplishments of this first graduating class. Our missions pastor, Jay Hoff, personally hands out diplomas, congratulating each graduate by name.

Finally, my friend Joseph calls me to the front. He tells the great assembly about our church. He tells them about his visit to our town. About the people he met in California. He asks my traveling companions to stand. And then he invites me to address the Graduating Class of 2009.

"My friends, honored guests, Class of 2009, I give you Pastor Matthew Cork!"

I do not know that I have ever felt what I felt at that moment any other time in my life. I wonder sometimes if I will ever feel it again. As I approached that microphone under the starry skies of Andhra Pradesh and the bright lights, it was as though God had prepared me my entire life for this single occasion.

I look at my handwritten notes. Ballpoint blue ink on lined paper. I take a deep breath. I look up into the lights at the large crowd, and at my friends Joseph and Mariam, and at the students seated up front.

"In twenty years we may be more disappointed by the things we did not do than by the things we did. But in twenty years, we will look back on this day and not be disappointed!"

I look up at the students in light blue robes; their bright eyes look back from under their mortarboard caps. They are in tune, giving me eye contact, smiling broadly. I continue.

"Today we are a part of history. Today, because of your courage, perseverance, and dedication to the Dalits and the call of God on your life—eternity is going to be different!

"Dr. D'souza, OM staff, principals, teachers, thank you! Thank you for not just teaching about Christ but actually being the hands and feet of Christ. You inspire, challenge, and motivate us all to follow Him with greater zeal, love, and commitment. And as we dedicate these graduates, we thank you: for your passion and your desire have made this moment possible. These great-looking students: their lives, and ours, will be forever changed.

"Proverbs 31:8 and 9 says this: 'Speak up for those who cannot speak for themselves; ensure justice for those being crushed. Yes, speak up for the poor and helpless, and see that they get justice' [NLT].

"Today is a step toward justice. Your voice has spoken loudly for those who previously had no voice.

"As you celebrate this one step towards freedom, you take this giant leap into a new world. You have now been given power by the living God to give away this hope; to change your community with your education, and to tell the world of this one Savior Jesus Christ. God Almighty has given you this freedom.

"We are counting on you. We are so proud of your accomplishment today. It will be recorded in the history books of India. It will change the face of eternity forever!

"Step forth with courage. Hold your head high. You are created in the image of the almighty God. He will use you for greater things than you could ever imagine.

"So, we dedicate you in the name of the Father, Son, and Holy Spirit. I pray the prayer Paul prayed to the church in Ephesus, 'Now to Him who is able to do exceedingly, abundantly above all that we ask or think, according to the power that works in us, to Him be glory in the church by Christ Jesus to all generations'" [Ephesians 3:20–21 NKJV].

And as strongly as I believe those words apply to these students, they also apply to me.

At the close of the ceremony, a young girl grabs me by the arm. I recognize her immediately. I met her in Pipe Village, two years before. She is wearing her bright blue cap and gown. Her tassel has been turned. Tonight, she is a graduate. In English, she introduces me to her mother and her grandfather. They have tears in their eyes. They look approvingly at their graduate. I can feel the swell of parental pride.

> Her tassel has been turned. She introduces me to her mother and her grandfather. They have tears in their eyes.

They turn to me and say, "Thank you, Pastor Matthew." They reach out to shake my hand. "Tell your good people in California, too. Tell them we said, 'Thank you.'"

I am humbled. I do not deserve this. I tell them I will deliver their message.

Three generations. They taste freedom. They embrace hope. They know the source. Someone takes a picture. Grandpa, Mom, graduate, and me. I cherish that photograph. It declares the freedom we have all worked so hard to achieve.

With the graduation finally over and its residual emotions still lingering, we continue with our trip. The producer of *Not Today*, along with Brent Martz and his team, traveled with me to Hyderabad and the historic graduation, and then proceeded on to trace the steps of our main character, Caden, through the streets of Kolkata, Mumbai, and beyond. They are on the hunt for film locations. They also capture the graduation ceremony and create an amazing video short for our folks back home.

Our team goes on after the graduation to visit several of our schools and search out locations for new campus sites. The momentum toward Joseph's dream of building one thousand schools is gathering steam.

It has been hard work, all-consuming work. For our Indian friends, obviously. But for us as well. I am overjoyed, yet I am completely spent.

There is a Dickensian irony in the timing. It is the best of times. It is the worst of times. My calendar had never been more crowded. My trip to India came two weeks before launch Sunday. It was all closing in, all good. There were moments when I wondered if I could I go on.

When I get back to my office in California, my calendar is crammed. I am exhausted. Now, however, is not the time for rest.

Chapter 12

COMMITMENT

UPON RETURNING from India, we put the finishing touches on our planning for the launch. There are still meetings with leadership and donors. Our staff is in high gear.

I have never felt such exhaustion. It is like the final leg of a marathon. And yet, energy comes from somewhere unseen. It keeps me going. I have never been in this zone before. Every morning, I wake up with a start. I greet God. I am ready to go.

The critics let their objections be known. I receive emails that express opposition; some of it personal. But many more express full and wholehearted support in countless ways. There are tough issues to settle on the way to the jam-packed weekend. But in spite of the long meetings and the sometime contentious decision making, I have a quiet strength and peace and confidence that I have never known before. It surpasses understanding.

And in the whirlwind, the date arrives. Commitment Weekend comes. It begins on Saturday night. As usual, I arrive early. I pray with our worship team. They are giddy with enthusiasm. I mingle with folks as they file in. The big room fills. The stage is set, the red Global Freedom logo front and center. High-energy music fills the air. It is happening. I whisper a prayer of thanks for what He taught me then that prepares me for my situation today.

"WE SPEAK TO NATIONS . . ."

We repeat the service twice more on Sunday morning. It is a large attendance for all three services. Dr. D'souza has flown in from India. We embrace heartily at the front row.

As I see him, and he greets me with his warm "Matthew, my good brother!" I reflect on our amazing journey that brings us to this weekend. His vision for Dalit freedom and education rooted in the liberating power of the Gospel of Jesus Christ had not only impacted a nation, but it has changed me. It has transformed our church. Two weeks prior, he welcomed me before those graduating students and teachers and parents and grandparents, in the courtyard of a newly constructed school in the heart of India. Now I introduce him once more to thousands of folks who are inspired by his work. Emotion wells up in me again as we meet at the front of the worship center.

Three times we bring our message to a large audience. The first hour Sunday morning remains most vivid in my memory. It is the service that includes our middle school and high school crowd. They fill the wings on either side with banners and placards. For weeks, they have prepared for this moment. Most carry a tubular container in one hand, brightly colored with Global Freedom printed on the side. It is their "Live Simply So Others Can Simply Live" bank. They have skipped snacks and CDs and the purchase of video games and designer clothes and visits to the movie theater and put the proceeds of these "sacrifices" aside, depositing the cash through the slots at the top. Today, they are prepared to turn their contributions over to Global Freedom's cause. The excitement in this new generation is palpable. It fills the room. *We are empowering tomorrow's generation today,* I think as I scan the wings of the auditorium filled with chattering teenagers.

As folks file in to their seats, I see the marked envelopes in hand, right there with their notebooks and Bibles. Our people are prepared with their pledges. They have considered the cause, considered the cost, prayed about their participation, and now they are ready to give.

Our worship team begins with Israel Houghton's challenge. *"We speak to nations. We speak to strongholds..."*

"Be broken!"

A video starts. A husband and wife speak of triumph in the tragedy of the debilitating illness of their son. A maturing adult tells about his journey as a high school sponsor and how it has transformed him. Then a young couple, Scott and Andrea Sward, barely recovering, tell about their commitment to go to Cambodia on a mission to serve Jesus. In the pursuit of that calling, just months before, on an interstate highway in Colorado, they suffered a terrible, unavoidable automobile accident. They both were injured, Andrea seriously. In the horrible collision and twisted metal and shattered glass, they lost their precious little boy, Isaac. Just after his first birthday. As they share, their gracious spirit of deep grief blended with secure hope touch us all via the video message. They are still on their way to Cambodia, they say. The unscheduled, life-altering incident has not derailed their determination to serve.

As I welcome the folks, there is a high sense of anticipation, exhilaration, and enthusiasm permeating the place. If "enthusiasm," which literally means "God in us" is it, then the entire room itself is enthusiastic. God is present. I learned a long time ago that omnipresence means that God is always here. Everywhere. All of the time. The question is this: "Are we aware?" When a large crowd comes together like this and they are corporately aware, altogether tuned in, there is nothing like it. God shows up.

And it is true for me. I have been preaching Sunday after Sunday for a long time. But on this occasion, there is a freedom I had not known before. The energy comes from somewhere unseen. The words flow easily. The passion fills up the words and phrases. There is credibility, not in the messenger but in the message itself. It is a moment of truth. I stand in the dock along with everyone else. This is not just for them; it is for me, too.

We cover a lot of ground. We go back to the prophets Haggai and Zechariah. We identify with their pathos, the tragedy when Israel abandoned a passion for God. They allowed the temple to fall into ruin. Then, they yawned in apathy when the prophets called for a rebuilding, for renewal. The prophets also declared the promise that God would bless them if they would only turn back, lay down their selfish pursuits, and align themselves with God's purposes in the world.

> The two sides of the globe connect. We are far away, but we are one.

For a few moments, I almost feel like Zechariah himself, lost in the message of restoration. It is as though we are at the intersection of need and supply. The two sides of the globe connect. We meet each other's needs. It is give-and-take both ways. We are far away, but we are one.

I tell everyone that Mardi and I are in agreement on our own pledge. It is a God-sized stretch for us, but we stand together. We had prayed over our pledge card. For starters, we sold our extra car on Craigslist in a single day. The cash proceeds go to Global Freedom.

Peggy, a registered nurse, comes to the platform with her friend and colleague at the hospital, Karen. Peggy had been avoiding God for decades. In an easy manner, Karen talked about her life with God. Peggy was intrigued. Karen invited her to come to church a few months back. But it wasn't until Christmas Eve that the power of the incarnation got hold of her. She choked back the emotion as she told our people about how God drew her irresistibly to Himself that night. She is reborn. Forever changed.

Then, we fire up another video. Marco, in his own voice, tells us that five years ago, his life on Cypress Street in the next town over was filled with "drugs and drinking and fighting and gang violence and sex with girls I didn't even know." But then a group of high school kids start showing up in the neighborhood to play soccer and basketball to build friendships. They laugh and tease and have fun. Marco felt accepted, affirmed. They invite him to a baseball game at Angel Stadium. Then they invite him to church. In time, he lets down his guard and listens as kids his own age talk about new life. About forgiveness. About wholeness. About hope. About real freedom. About Jesus. He opens his heart. Marco, and Cypress Street, will never be the same.

Then, I introduce the man who has become an associate pastor to our people. "Folks, please welcome my good friend and partner in the Gospel, give him a warm welcome . . . Dr. Joseph D'souza!" Standing ovation. We embrace again.

"I want to tell you about a man who visited India two hundred years ago," Joseph begins. He speaks about a cobbler from England with an unmatched curiosity. As a boy, the Brit studied Greek. He was fascinated with the tales of the British East India Company. He was young, but felt an unmistakable call to bring the good news to that exotic, faraway continent, as he called it. His Church of England turned him down. The church leaders considered him a renegade. He convinced the Danes to give him a legitimate visa, and with that authorization moved to Calcutta. While there, he mastered Hebrew to match the biblical Greek, and went on to learn twelve Indian dialects including Sanskrit and Hindi.

The missionary won a few converts. Not many. But he established institutions—schools, hospitals, and clinics. His primary accomplishment was to translate the Bible into several Indian languages. Those translations have been printed, reprinted, distributed, and read for two centuries all over the great land of India.

"That was two hundred years ago," Dr. D'souza says. "Today, I stand before you as the product of his courageous, unlikely ministry. If not for this man, the son of a cobbler, I would not know Christ, I would not have the life I live today, I would not be committed to the freedom of the Dalit people of India, if not for the work and sacrifice of William Carey, the father of modern missions." He goes on to tell us that on the anniversary of two hundred years since Carey's arrival in India, all of India celebrated his contribution to the Indian nation with a commemorative stamp. It is a fine gesture.

But Carey's real legacy is Global Freedom, D'souza declares. Today, thanks to the seeds planted by William Carey, the liberating power of the Gospel is impacting lives exponentially. It is changing the face of a nation and the destiny of 250 million Dalits.

"I wish William Carey could be here in this room today," D'souza says. "Wow. It would, as you Americans like to say, blow his mind!" Laughter fills the room.

"We are partners. I thank God for you."

Dr. D'souza finishes. I thank him and step to the microphone. It's time.

"WHY NOT TODAY?"

"So now, I have a question for you. It is a serious question." The silence was penetrating.

"Why not today?"

I invite everyone to take a stand. "We are in this together," I say as I look across the crowded room. Everyone is eager, especially our students. It is a sacred moment of commitment, right here in God's presence. I read them one of my favorite quotes from John Ortberg. He talks about how a commitment to step out for God is almost always accompanied by fear. "If you have not known this fear," Ortberg says, "there's a real good chance you have been sitting in a chair too long."

It is time to get out of the chair, I say.

And they do. I stand and watch. Up in the balcony; over on the wings, left and right. Down the center aisle, they come. Bearing their gifts. In their freedom, they bring the possibility of freedom to others.

The worship team is in their place. The drummer taps the beat. The musicians begin. It is an incredibly perfect lyric, from the heart of Sara Groves. It is called "When the Saints" from her album *Tell Me What You Know.*

I do not believe I am capable of explaining what it means to me to see our families come together like this. Husbands and wives and children, old and young, some alone, others with friends, high school students and collegians, many with tears all come toward the front to the amazing strains of Sara's music. "Lord, I have a heavy burden of all I've seen and know..."[1]

She sings of Paul and Silas in prison, and their song of freedom; of Moses in Pharaoh's court; of the Underground Railroad where those enslaved escaped to follow a compelling dream of freedom; the missionaries who laid down their lives at the point of a spear; Mother Teresa at the bedside of the dying in Calcutta.

And then Jesus, on the road to Calvary. "When the saints go marching in," Sara sings, "I want to be one of them."

I watch as the saints march forward. It is not an envelope or a bank with coins rattling or a check written. It is a vision caught. It is the awareness that I matter. What I think. What I resolve. What I do. It matters. What we commit to together, husband and wife, mother and father, businessperson, professional, laborer, builder, clerk, administrator, educator, son or daughter, wealthy or paycheck-to-paycheck.

Together they say: I count. I can turn away from the things that hold me back. I can be a part. I can withhold or I can give. I can tune out or I can listen. I can make excuses or I can affirm the truth. I can step back or I can step forward. It is up to me.

I stand there as a silent observer. English speakers. Spanish speakers. These are people with open hearts. Open minds. Stepping out. Stepping forward.

These are the saints. They are marching in.

When I landed in Hyderabad after an all-night flight at the old, broken-down airport and was accosted for the first time by India's street kids; when I learned something of the plight of the "untouchables" at Pipe Village and in the slums; when Dr. D'souza explained what has happened in the last decade to break through impenetrable barriers; when I came to understand the transforming power of the Gospel on the other side of planet Earth; well, it all crushed in on me that night in the Corporate Stay Hotel. I came face-to-face with a challenge so great, so heartbreaking, so insolvable, that God broke through to me.

It changed me forever.

That was 2009. What I understand now is that I was given a gift. It is the gift of vision. It is a clear exposure to the things that are close to the heart of God. It has given me a sense of purpose and direction and energy that I had not known before. I know more change is coming. I welcome the process of transformation in my life. It is like being hungry and thirsty, and finding a banquet table and cool clean water all at the same time.

Our folks are finding it, too.

NOTE

1. Sara Groves, "When the Saints," *Tell Me What You Know*, Sponge Records 2007.

Chapter 13

TODAY

THAT OUR CHURCH WOULD PRODUCE a theatrical film was, frankly, beyond my wildest imagination. And I can safely say neither our leadership nor our congregation ever thought of it either.

But people who think outside the box are people I like to be around. Innovation and creativity are essential to fresh, energized approaches to vision casting, problem solving, and resource mobilizing. We believe it's good to take risks. We now think of innovation as "riskovation."

As I explained earlier, *Not Today* was born as Global Freedom emerged as a movement in our church. It came out of the context of a new wave of faith-based films made by people just like us, and then an Oscar-winning film that captured a worldwide audience, *Slumdog Millionaire*. On that watershed afternoon, Brent and I imagined the making of a full-length feature film that would advance the cause of Dalit freedom.

It would change our lives.

The title *Not Today* says so much. Most of us are caught up in our own issues. Even when confronted with irrefutable evidence of a terrible injustice, we would rather just turn aside and move on. The heavy burden of engaging the challenge is too much. We will say, "Not today," as though we will pick it up later when we have more time. And that's exactly how injustice spreads, from a neighborhood to a region to a province or a state to a nation to the globe. It is more than procrastination; it is a kind of blatant denial. We see it. We turn away. And the problem gets worse.

But when a vision really captures us, denial turns to affirmation. Neglect converts to focus. *Yes. This is a problem. Yes. I will do something. Not tomorrow. Not next month or next year or after I'm done with everything else. Not someday. But today.* Yes. Today.

Today *is* the day. And on that memorable afternoon, in Brent's office, we made that determination: *Not Today* would begin—today.

FICTION—BUT NOT REALLY

We scoped out movie sites and visited the red-light districts in Kolkata and Mumbai. Brent and the crew walked the streets and spoke with freedom fighters, unsung heroes, workers who assisted in rescuing trafficked women and children.

I saw the original version of the script for *Not Today* at the first graduation of the high school class in Hyderabad. We loved the story from the start. In many ways, it was our story. We live in Orange County, widely recognized as one of the wealthiest in America. We are like Caden Welles—too often obsessed with protecting what we have, imagining that our world reflects the rest of the world, skeptical of traditional religious solutions and overblown piety, rarely venturing beyond the comforts of our own neighborhoods. When we do, it is too often on a flight off to a resort that lives up to our high standard. We know little of the emerging world, other than what we see on our high-definition wide screens from our overstuffed lounge chair, enveloped by surround sound and shaken only by powered subwoofers. If we even take the time to watch the news, we understand little, though somehow, we relish our confident belief that we have it all figured out. We don't even see it when tragedy lives right next door, much less on the other side of the globe.

But out there beyond our comfort zone, there are too many Annikas. Too many Kirans. Too many Ashas (another child in the film). All it may take is a toss of a dart to bring us, unwilling, face-to-face with heartbreaking realities. And when we engage, even without intent or purpose, something powerful happens. It's a transformation of the heart. An awakening of the spirit. A rescuing of the soul.

> Yes, it is fiction. But not really. Like this main character, we are unaware that in the rest of the world, we Americans are known for our air of superiority.

We loved our little documentary, *Deletes*. But we loved the idea of a dramatic film even more. Yes, it is fiction. But not really. It is a story we enter into.

We connect. We connect with characters. We feel what they feel. We connect with Caden's indifference and the calloused detachment of his three happy-go-lucky pals. Like this main character (a young, privileged resident of upscale Newport Beach), we are unaware that in the rest of the world, we Americans are known for our smug air of superiority, our perpetual demand for instant gratification, and our ready capacity to point out the inadequacies of cultures not our own. We connect with Caden's mother, Sarah—her postdivorce struggle, her heartfelt desire for her son to embrace a strong faith that is all his own. She wants him to experience the adventure of a far-off land, and yet she fears the worst. Annika captures our hearts—her wide-eyed curiosity, her playful self-reliance, her street smarts, her love for and dependence on her father. Her innocence lost as she is sold away. We try to imagine her life on the street. We connect with Annika's father, Kiran, who tries so hard to provide; but even his most intentional efforts seem futile in a world with so little economic possibility and so many present dangers. We grieve with him in despair as Annika disappears.

Young women will understand Audrey's conflict as she feels a deep love for her boyfriend, Caden, but at the same time, holds on to a bitter aversion toward his self-absorbed duplicity and his disregard for her sensibilities. The story takes us into the slums, up and down the crowded streets where Dalits are caught in a meaningless, powerless existence. Cruelty is commonplace. Hopelessness reigns. Cinema powerfully draws us in. We share the need for prayer as our characters face disappointment, conflict, fears, and loss.

THE PIECES COME TOGETHER

After that initial look at the script, there were several reviews and a couple of rewrites. But now, it was ready. We understood that we would need all the volunteer efforts we could find. On-location shoots, background actors, staging, lighting, sound, editing—all a massive undertaking. A prayer team began in earnest and has sustained us through today.

We developed a timeline and a budget. We believed both were realistic, doable. We were wrong.

Early in the process, we met Chris and Denise Bueno, who had a company called Carmel Entertainment. They brought their experience in assisting in the distribution of the Sherwood films (*Facing the Giants* and *Fireproof*) to the screen. They looked at our script and heard the story of Global Freedom and jumped right in with their encouragement and network of friends.

With their help, we agreed that we should have the best actors available for our lead roles. Beverly Holloway is a casting director with nearly fifty major films to her credit. She read the script and joined us. Within weeks, hundreds of actors signed up to read.

Brent and his team went to Century City to meet with potential actors for the roles of Caden, his friends, Audrey, Sarah, and Luke. Brent's enthusiasms were high as he heard his script read aloud by professional, card-carrying (Screen Actors Guild) actors. The words came to life. The dialogue is engaging and filled with pathos.

After several weeks of auditions, Cody Longo was selected for the lead role as Caden; John Schneider as Caden's stepdad, Luke; Cassie Scerbo as Caden's girlfriend, Audrey; Shari Rigby as Caden's mother, Sarah; Walid Amini as Annika's father, Kiran; and in India, young Persis Karen was selected from hundreds of Dalit students at the Good Shepherd School in Hyderabad to play the key role of Annika.

The script called for filming in Newport Beach, Yorba Linda, and India. Three homes emerged, one a fabulous house on the bluff overlooking Balboa Island in the Newport Harbor, donated by a former member of our church who relocated near the beach. Its disappearing pool, wide deck, and open living room were perfect for our opening scene where Caden, Bill, Z-Roy, and Eli toss the dart during a poker game over beer and cigars that determines their plan to go to India on a lark. It would be this year's annual party junket. Audrey confronts Caden that night for his duplicity. It was a perfect setting for the scene.

Another church member loaned us his bright-red Enzo Ferrari, a twelve-cylinder, 650-horsepower Berlinetta with gull-wing doors, one of only four hundred built in Italy in 2003. Capable of speeds over two hundred fifty miles per hour, it was the perfect way to communicate to our audience that Caden's father was wealthy, and that his life of privilege knew no bounds. Of course, Cody loved driving up to the house in that car, and on the day we filmed the scene, an exuberant crowd watched just outside camera range.

MOVIEMAKING IN A MONSOON

Joseph D'souza's India team rallied around our project, including The Johnny Lever Film Company (our production services company in India) and Beena Rao, who played a pivotal role. We knew that there would be resistance to our project as there was for Danny Boyle when he directed and produced *Slumdog Millionaire*. We pulled together our crew for on-location shooting in Hyderabad, Goa, and Mumbai. It was a massive project. The count for cast and crew was thirty. They would leave Los Angeles mid-January 2010. Everyone cleared their calendars, lodging and meals arranged, film sites selected—Brent and the team were ready to go.

Just a few days before departure, competent people had worked to secure the necessary paperwork. But at the last minute, we were informed that we did not have proper permits from the Indian government. Our team went in high gear to rescue our plans, but to no avail. We were forced to cancel the six-week filming trip.

It took nine months to resolve the problem. Our prayer team moved into overdrive. The Johnny Lever Company managed to secure our permits. By God's grace, with permission granted (including a governmental review of the script), the doors opened for a July departure. It was the monsoon season.

> The rain seemed to serve as a fitting mood for our story. Annika's tears mingled with the raindrops on her cheeks.

Yes, filming in India is challenging. Add to that, bad weather. Rain definitely was not in the script. It made for difficult travel, building of sets, and movement in scenes. But Brent and Jon, our writer and director, were philosophical. Rain has long been a cinematic symbol of oppression, sadness, and grief. We knew we were dealing with the plight of an entire people group who have suffered for three thousand years under the cruelest sort of injustice and mistreatment. The rain seemed to serve as a fitting mood for our story. Annika would run lost through the rain, finding her friend Asha, lifeless, cold, and wet under a plastic tarp, callously left on a trash heap. Annika's tears would mingle with the raindrops on her cheeks. Perfect.

While the delay was costly and a disappointment to us all, it appeared that God had a plan that was much better than ours to communicate the reality of our story.

The filming, shot by Abraham Martinez, would last twenty-one days and take our crew from the slums in Hyderabad to a train through the countryside on to Goa and Mumbai. Our team faced daily challenges, sometimes being removed from sites during filming, sometimes thinking there was permission when there was not, dealing with Bollywood technicians who had their own way of working, coping with illness that spread through the cast and crew, and finally meeting deadlines on a limited budget. Through it all, our people worked very hard and kept spirits high—learning to lean on God's grace, to trust without reservation and deliver powerful performances.

Many on our crew had never experienced anything close to our time in India. Most had never set foot on this faraway subcontinent. The smells, the food, the humidity, the slums were all new. But there was something else, too, something even more basic. They had never seen such dependence on God, such a heart for hurting people; they did not anticipate the warmth and beauty of the Indian people, in spite of difficult circumstances. They were part of a powerful cause. They got close to God's heart. Our crew was deeply affected by the power of our project. We all became believers on a whole new level.

Our two main characters, Caden and Kiran, move through the city streets and at night into the dark shadows of brothels looking for Annika. They meet despicable characters that traffic in human slavery, calloused ruffians who know nothing of justice or mercy or kindness. At last, with twenty thousand dollars wired to them from Luke in California via Western Union, now converted to cold cash, Caden pays off Devika Tomar. She is a front woman for the slave trade who poses as a café owner. The money is a bribe to find Annika somewhere in Mumbai. She takes Caden and the cash in a random taxi to an industrial center, which he later learns is a hidden central terminal for India's burgeoning trafficking trade. Our crew had to complete that final scene in record time. Shortly after the final moments were captured, the entire crew was escorted back to the airport to head for home.

Time and money both ran out.

But the filming was complete.

INTO POSTPRODUCTION

We celebrated the accomplishment. But that celebration was short-lived. The real work was about to begin. Late every night, both in Orange County and India, Brent and Jon viewed the day's work on a high-definition monitor. We had our challenges. For example, because we did not have proper monitors on the India shoot, a full 40 percent of our film was out of focus and unusable. In spite all that, we were all pleased with the results. Abraham's shots were stunning. The India landscape, the street scenes both in daylight and at night were realistic and compelling. But now, the great task of compiling those scenes into a story with forward momentum, twist and turns, and—most important—heart would begin.

The first working draft by Jon and Brent emerged from their studio-caliber equipment. It totaled a full two-and-a-half hours from opening scene to final fade. Way too long. That's when Jon Van Dyke introduced Brent to Jeff Wishengrad, known as a high-demand postproduction editor.

"That's really good work," he told the director and producer. "Now, let's make it better."

And he did. When I saw the finished product, cut to just over ninety minutes, my eyes widened. Same film. Same story. Same characters. Same scenes. But Jeff's editing added power, punch, and realism.

Next, soundtrack. Enter Don Harper. Brent was acquainted with Don's incomparable work. There are too many credits to name, but when I heard that Harper had worked with Disney on *Tarzan* and *Lion King,* and that he is credited as arranger/composer for *August Rush, National Treasure* (and *National Treasure: Book of Secrets*), and the *Sorcerer's Apprentice,* I couldn't imagine that he would take on *Not Today.* He did.

Don's score captures the heartbeat of India, the raw emotion of the loss of a little girl to trafficking, the electric action of the chase scenes, the intensity of malicious encounters in the dark underworld of lost children, the depth of feeling in Sarah's prayer, the sheer joy of friendship and reunion, all of it, in a potent undercurrent of melody and rhythm that does not distract but enhances. The musical score, which features the matchless violin of Charlie Bisharat, draws you into the strength of the story in a seamless stream of energy moving us forward toward conviction and action.

PREMIERE!

It was time to share our film with the people who made it happen. When we launched the Global Freedom campaign, we knew it was for the Dalit children of India. We would build schools. We would support safe houses for the escapees of human trafficking. We would find support for students to sustain them from matriculation through graduation. We knew we found a viable partner in Dr. D'souza. But we did not know we would produce a full-length feature film.

From the start, our leadership and our people had supported this unlikely venture. Sure, there were some who questioned the project. They were there from the start, and some are still there. But the great majority understood our purpose, believed in our people, and stood by us with their prayers, their support, and their encouragement. It was time to share the finished film, first with them.

We rented the largest theater in our town for the premiere, inviting our staff and all the people who had volunteered and worked on the project. It became the most coveted invitation I can remember. People lined up an hour before the showing. Joseph D'souza was there.

Before we began, as I stepped before the full house with Brent and Joseph beside me, the folks broke out in sustained applause. I waved it off, pointing back to them and then the creative team, and then reminding them that this was God's project, and that He deserved all the praise. The whole scene filled me with a level of gratitude I cannot describe.

I spoke of my enormous pride in Brent and Jon for their tireless efforts, which stood as a model for the hundreds and hundreds of people who gave, volunteered, served, and prayed on both sides of the globe. We all agreed, if we had known the obstacles, the volume and pressures of the work, the delays, the surprises, the disappointments, the moments of complete and utter confusion, none of us would have signed up. It was an intense journey. But it put us all squarely in the middle of this movement of God. Liberation is happening. The lives of Dalit children and families and villages and neighborhoods are, by God's grace, being transformed. The dark power of casteism is losing its grip. A nation is being turned upside down.

As a result, God's work in India is spilling over on Orange County, too. The hundreds of Americans who never imagined they would know India's good people as friends, as brothers and sisters, have come back home to this country with a new sense of vision and purpose. Our strategic partners have been energized in new ways. Joseph took to the microphone and spoke with enthusiasm over the power of the film, *Not Today*. With eloquence, he expressed his conviction that this film will be a significant catalyst in taking the movement to a whole new level.

> It was an intense journey. But it put us all squarely in the middle of this movement of God. Liberation is happening.

The lights dimmed. The movie began.

I listened afterward as our people described their experience at that premiere. They told me that the mood in the room was electric with anticipation. "You could hear a pin drop," they said, in those intense moments of drama. You heard sniffs as Sarah agonized over her son's reckless pursuit of a little girl through the dark corners and dangerous streets of unknown crowded cities on the other side of the world. You could feel the tension between Caden and his stepdad, Luke, as they squared off, putting Sarah in the middle of their conflict. When Annika's father, Karin, comes to terms with what might happen to his little girl as a result of his action, the crowd slipped into his anguish. And then, on the train, as Karin goads his arrogant traveling companion Caden with the question, "Where are you going to go? Disneyland?" everyone laughed out loud.

Up until the final scene, the several hundred people who filled the theater for that premiere sat rapt, caught up in the story and our actors' fine performances. Caden (Cody Longo) is convincing as the privileged American who transforms from indifference to compassion. Audrey (Cassie Scerbo), the hyperspiritual young Christian transforms from pesky, pious, and righteous girlfriend to caring supporter. Sarah (Shari Rigby) shines as a conflicted mom who wants the very best for her maverick son. Kiran (Walid Amini) grows from streetwise but lost untouchable to loving, trusting father. And Annika (Persis Karen), who was lost, is ultimately found. Our audience was ready to stand up and cheer.

The film ends with a haunting close-up of Annika (Persis) that just plain nails the finish. Against a pure white backdrop, she looks away pensively. Don Harper's score rivets us to the little girl who would otherwise have been lost to a horrific life of slavery, but now, thankfully, she is found. She is free. Numbed by her own painful journey, she slowly turns to the camera and looks directly into our eyes. As she does, a hint of a smile forms on the edge of her lips, and our throat thickens and warm emotion wells up inside us. We are hooked. We'll do whatever it takes.

As we all left the theater that memorable night, one lesson was clear. We still needed some serious work on the ending. As we celebrate Annika's release, we wanted to design a clear, direct challenge to everyone who sees the film to get involved.

Our creative team rolled up their sleeves.

TO JOIN A MOVEMENT

Brent contacted Cody, Cassie, Walid, and Shari. They were enthusiastic. By now, each had been deeply touched by the plight of the Dalit people, Joseph's vision, the power of the Dalit Education Centers to transform, the injustice of casteism, and the belief that we can make a difference. Yes, each said they would gladly speak out.

Brent returned to India with a cameraman and found Persis on the playground at the Good Shepherd School in Hyderabad. If you had not seen the film, you would consider her just another of the kids in uniform, excited about learning, practicing English, reading books, and working out problems and filling in the blanks on pages of homework. But we know otherwise. With no acting experience, Persis will win a place in the hearts of theatergoers around the world. The camera follows Brent across the playground as a collection of young Dalit students kick soccer balls and chase one another in games of tag. He takes Persis under his arm, and challenges us to be a part of a movement that will change the world.

As the film comes to a close, there is indeed something to cheer. While Asha lost her life to trafficking, Annika is rescued. She returns to her father's loving embrace. Some of the traffickers are brought to justice. What we do matters. We can make a difference. Listen to Caden and Audrey and Sarah and Kiran. Look into Annika's eyes. You will consider the meaning of your own life.

Like all of us, you will want to do something.

Throughout the process of making the film, we knew we would find distribution partners. We have been encouraged by the organizations and government agencies that share our conviction that something must be done. This is a global problem too long neglected.

In 2010, Pulitzer Prize–winning journalists Nicholas Kristof and Sheryl WuDunn wrote a compelling, disturbing book that served as a wake-up call to American journalists who have neglected the reality of global slavery. *Half the Sky: Turning Oppression into Opportunity for Women Worldwide* has sparked a whole new level of awareness. PBS aired a powerful documentary based on the book.

According to pollsters, our emerging generation of young people may be leaving the church in record numbers, but they are passionate about impacting the global economy in ways that rescue, prevent, and restore the victims of trafficking. Law schools are focusing on international law and human rights. I'm proud to say that churches like ours are looking hard at the teachings of Jesus and coming to the same conclusion as we did: God's heart breaks over the plight of the poor and neglected. Jesus calls us to seek out the lost until they are found.

In 2012, *Not Today* received four cinema awards, including best breakthrough performance by an actress, Persis Karen, at the Monaco Charity Film Festival.

Brent has taken the film to audiences across the country. In private viewings, we have gathered information from focus groups, partners in the cause, film distributors, and film festivals. I'm proud to say we have come away with enthusiasm and high marks, including four awards (so far). In 2012, *Not Today* received four cinema awards: best picture at the Dixie Film Festival, best narrative feature at the Pan Pacific Film Festival, redemptive storyteller at the Redemptive Film Festival, and best breakthrough performance by an actress, Persis Karen, at the Monaco Charity Film Festival.

Our convictions became reality when Lionsgate and EMI offered to be our distribution partners. Now, as we prepare for a nationwide theatrical release, our prayer is simple. It has not changed. This is not about us. It is more than a movie. It's about God's work. It is simple obedience. Solomon put it like this: "Speak up for those who cannot speak for themselves, for the rights of all who are destitute. Speak up and judge fairly; defend the rights of the poor and needy."[1]

I was not prepared for the response that would become a global enterprise, with a life all its own. What seemed like audacity is becoming a reality.

The cause is becoming a movement.

NOTE

1. Proverbs 31:8–9.

Chapter 14

EMANCIPATE!

ON THAT WATERSHED 2001 day in New Delhi in Bhawan Stadium, something powerful was unleashed. As an Indian Christian minister, Joseph D'souza affirmed freedom of religion for India's Dalit population. He declared, along with his friend Udit Raj, that every person comes into the world with the same basic rights as everyone else. Today, Joseph will tell you, as firm as his conviction might be, he did not anticipate that so many would join him in the cause.

In our country, we are stirred every time we hear our national anthem, with its reminder that the United States flag waves "o'er the land of the free." And then, whenever we hear *"Let freedom ring!"* it calls us back to the Liberty Bell, which may be cracked, but still resonates with us Americans because it calls out something embedded deep within our souls. It is that universal longing to be free.

And in our tradition, traced back to the early debates so vigorously argued at the dawn of our nation's history, freedom is the essence of what binds us together. We fight and die for it. Our national cemeteries honor those who paid the ultimate sacrifice to ensure that we stay free.

I believe that freedom goes back further in history, to Jesus Himself, who understood His role as liberator. He came, as He put it, to set the captive free. He said, "If the Son sets you free, you will be free indeed."[1]

Jesus understood this basic yearning that was planted into the human spirit from the time of creation. Something has gone tragically wrong with our world—Jesus called it sin. Sin happens on a personal level. It also is systemic, when greed and power and abuse become woven into the fabric of the social order. Thugs take control of the streets, where vulnerable people made in the image of God are drugged and then bought and sold like cattle. Out-of-control governments become masterminds of genocide. Ruthless and unethical tyrants raid business profits to enrich themselves at the expense of the people who created the profits in the first place. Jesus understood this longing of the human heart to be free, and He offers a freedom that transcends every manner of evil.

In 2004, the popular Christian band Caedmon's Call went to India and was captured by the same vision that captured me that night in the Corporate Stay Hotel. They did what artists do; as singer/songwriters they sketched out lyrics and then added a melody line, then filled in the tracks with rhythms and chords. They studied Indian sounds, adding an air of authenticity with *tablas* and the *sarod* and *sitar*. Then, they gathered to record in the studio. The result was a powerful series of songs that have become an anthem for Dalit freedom. Their collection is called *Share the Well*.

In the final cut, the "Dalit Hymn," they make a clarion call to the Indian government to pay attention to the evils of casteism and make the legislative changes that will be required to free the Dalit peoples (untouchables) of India. With a distinctly Indian beat and sound, they cry, "Emancipate! Emancipate! Prime Minister, Emancipate!"

Free the Dalits! is Caedmon's call. And little did they know, just two years later, the first Sikh prime minister of India, Manmohan Singh, made a breakthrough and clear comparison between that detestable governmental policy of apartheid that held South African blacks in bondage and India's untouchability, calling it a "unique discrimination" and a "blot on humanity." The prime minister heard the cry of Caedmon's Call (and many others), inspired by Moses: "Let my people go!"

The momentum is unstoppable.

In the spring of 2010, Joseph went to Cape Town, South Africa, where apartheid was finally declared illegal in 1991. Over four thousand leaders gathered there from nearly two hundred countries at the Third Lausanne Congress on World Evangelism. Dr. D'souza was asked to address a plenary session. He began by quoting Prime Minister Singh, and then the young potential prime minister and member of the Indian Parliament, Rahul Gandhi (born June 19, 1970). The son of Rajiv Gandhi, the sixth prime minister of India since independence from Great Britain, Rahul spoke out publicly, proclaiming that "casteism is worse than racism."

> Through the centuries, many Dalits have converted to Christianity only to find that the Christian church often continues to perpetuate the caste system.

A great irony, D'souza explained in his speech, is this: through the centuries, many Dalits have converted to Christianity only to find that the Christian church all too often continues to perpetuate the caste system. Dalits who followed Jesus because of His message of equality, justice, and reconciliation only found the continuation of the indignities of caste right there in the church—even among Christians who claim to follow this Jesus. Joseph's words were piercing and direct. In Jesus' kingdom (the church), the walls of cultural and ethnic barriers are to be broken down. In Jesus Christ, "there is neither Jew nor Gentile, neither slave nor free, nor is there male and female."[2]

Yet the Christian church in India has often acquiesced to the indignities and injustice of the ancient system of caste. To illustrate the point, D'souza referred to a BBC (South Asia) report from the town of Trichy in the southern state of Tamil Nadu. There, in a cemetery adjacent to an old Catholic church, is the unmistakable photograph of a cemetery in which Indian Christians are buried. Down the middle of the cemetery is a six-foot-high concrete wall that separates upper-caste Christians from "untouchable" Christians. Upper caste on one side of the wall; untouchables on the other. "Even in death," D'souza lamented, "on Christian church property for all to see, Dalits are forever reminded that they are contaminated."

This concrete wall of separation on church grounds is a lingering, disgraceful symbol of caste.

Back when Joseph addressed the huge gathering of Dalits in New Delhi who were declaring their break with Hinduism's grip back in 2001, he confessed that the church in his beautiful country remains guilty of perpetuating a cruel segregation and blatant discrimination against Dalits. He called it sin. He openly repented. He labeled it for what it is: a violation of Jesus' clear teaching. He choked with emotion. You could hear the sincerity in his voice and see it in his dampened eyes.

> D'souza told leaders that a new movement is emerging in India—people are discovering the Jesus of the Bible and gathering in new communities.

But now in Cape Town, Joseph proclaimed, there is clear evidence that the church in India still missed the message. The BBC report quotes Father Yesumariyan, a Jesuit lawyer and Dalit campaigner, who said on record, "Caste discrimination is rampant in the Catholic Church." Joseph called on leaders in Cape Town to work to end discrimination, especially where it still exists in the church of Jesus Christ.

D'souza told those leaders gathered in South Africa that a new movement is emerging in India—people are discovering the Jesus of the Bible and gathering in new communities in which the distinctions of caste are challenged. There is reconciliation, hope, healing, and building toward a future. The "creation myth" (as he described the nonbiblical tradition), taught for thousands of years, is the culture's justification for the system of caste. A new generation has resoundingly rejected that myth. The movement is unstoppable.

Pranitha Timothy, a lovely young woman who had once been sold into slavery and subject to unthinkable abuses, followed Joseph's address in Cape Town with a challenge to the same leaders. She found her way out from bondage. She now works to rescue and prevent trafficking in her native India. She is part of a worldwide effort to eradicate global slavery—the International Justice Mission. When Jesus announced His intent to set the captives free, said Pranitha, He was quoting the prophet Isaiah, who said, "The Lord has anointed me to proclaim good news to the poor. He has sent me to bind up the brokenhearted, to proclaim freedom for the captives and release from darkness for the prisoners" (Isaiah 61:1). Pranitha has seen it in her own life, and now in the lives of many others.

Slavery as an illegal global enterprise is highly profitable for its perpetrators, and in gross revenues is second only to illegal drug trafficking, Pranitha explained. She challenged her listeners at the Lausanne Congress to heed the words of the same prophet that Jesus quoted: "Learn to do right; seek justice. Defend the oppressed. Take up the cause of the fatherless; plead the case of the widow."

ADVOCATING FOR THE DALITS

Former Harvard professor Ana Aspra Steele now heads the Dalit Freedom Network, headquartered in Washington DC. DFN was launched to provide funding for Dalit Education Centers, schools that provide an English-language education for Dalit children. Their charge is to find sponsors in the United States who will support the children from the first year through high school. In addition to raising funds, under Dr. Steele's leadership, DFN has become a legislative advocacy organization, affecting legislators and policymakers in India and North America. DFN has made considerable advances in this arena. Dr. Steele puts it this way:

The aim of DFN's Social Justice Program is to address the deepest injustices that Dalits suffer, such as human trafficking and child and bonded labor, and to focus on strategic government advocacy to mitigate these crises. Although India has the necessary legislation in place to combat human trafficking and child labor, these atrocities continue largely unchallenged, and the ongoing toleration of these practices is recognized at the highest levels of the Indian judicial system. On November 15, 2008, in New Delhi, the Honorable Dr. Justice Arijit Pasayat of the Supreme Court of India stated that there was no bigger problem in India today than human trafficking. The United States and the international community can play an essential and constructive role in helping the Indian government to implement its anti-slavery and anti-child labor laws. The Social Justice team saw its first-ever legislative victory in 2007: House Concurrent Resolution 139 passed in the U.S. House of Representatives on July 24, 2007, expressing the sense of Congress that the United States should be committed to addressing the ongoing practice of "untouchability" with the Government of India. In the present Session of Congress, we are working on legislation that directly addresses the massive human trafficking of Dalits.

As of this writing, there are now 140 Dalit Education Center schools in operation, serving more than twenty-five thousand students. They are very much like the school I first visited at Uddamarri. Uniformed children line up, on time for class every day. They have an eagerness to learn. They practice their English. Our church has been responsible for building forty of these campuses. Our goals have not been reached, but we are well on our way.

The Tarika Women's Center in Bangalore is an example of how women, caught in the vise-grip of slavery, can be liberated and empowered to recover and rebuild a broken life. Women who escape indescribable abuse find safe haven at Tarika. They are welcomed, cared for, and fed. In the confines of this new community, there is counseling, education, job training, exercise, and nutrition. New skills develop in sewing, tailoring, embroidery, and even computer competencies. It is a safe environment filled with positive reinforcement, laughter, and dancing.

ROOPA'S TRANSFORMATION

In preparation for the release of our film, *Not Today*, I led a team of media people to India to show them firsthand what inspired the making of the movie and what we expect our film to fund. Our intent is for the proceeds of our movie to be used to promote the cause of Dalit freedom. That means we will continue to provide resources for both rescue and prevention. We will support safe houses like Tarika Women's Center and the Lydia Project in Hyderabad. We will build schools and provide support for students to receive an education from kindergarten through high school. Our media travel team included some eighteen journalists, media executives, and educators from all over the nation, including representatives from *Christianity Today*, CBN (the Christian Broadcasting Network), and Focus on the Family.

George Thomas, senior international reporter for CBN, traveled with us to India. We visited slums and schools in several cities, but it was the Tarika Women's Center that inspired a six-minute feature presentation that aired on CBN just weeks after our visit. Jeeva Kumar is director at the safe house, and she introduced our group to an attractive twentysomething, Roopa Raju. Along with the 105 women who completed the eighteen-month course as we observed the pomp and circumstance, Roopa graduated that same afternoon. It was a tearful, joyful ceremony.

Jeeva Kumar told George Thomas he must interview Roopa—her story would move us all. She was quite right. George set up his equipment—audio and video.

As a young girl, Roopa's parents sent her out of their shelter in the slum to be a "rag-picker." Reluctantly, she obeyed. She knew what that meant. Trash heaps piled up everywhere in her part of town, and children would wade through that refuse, picking and sifting, searching for anything of value to sell on the open market.

George had his camera rolling to record the interview. Roopa's Telegu language was translated, as her developing English fell short of detailing the nuances of her story. As a little girl working garbage dumps, she managed to eke out around a hundred rupees per day, just two dollars in American currency. But that wasn't enough. So her parents, Roopa continued, forced her to sleep with men to get additional money for the family. She became a prostitute.

In a voiceover, George described the interview: "With tears welling up in her eyes, Roopa described the rage she felt toward her parents." Remember, Roopa is a Dalit. Her anger toward her mother and father and her contempt for the system that enslaved her was evident as she shared her tortuous journey. But then, in the depth of her anguish, she found the Tarika Women's Center. There, she was counseled to think differently about her life and her future. Contrary to what she had been taught from childhood, she was not destined for a life of untouchability. Instead, she was made in the image of God and possessed full rights as a human being. The abuse must end, a new life begin. She had the power and the ability to choose a different path.

Roopa's eyes welled up with emotion. "I have forgiven my parents," she told her interviewer.

Roopa's study of the Bible opened her eyes to a new faith, a new community, and a new future. She entered the training at Tarika with high energy and determination.

On graduation day, not only were the media people from the United States in the audience, so were her parents. Jeeva made sure we knew the story. Tears rolled down her mother's and father's faces as Roopa walked across the stage wrapped in a brightly colored sari with a white sash identifying her accomplishment. She took her diploma from my friend Jay Hoff.

George asked Roopa's parents for their permission to interview them. "This is the proudest day of our lives," he father said in Telegu. Her mother nodded in agreement. Diploma under her arm, Roopa stepped up beside them, reaching for her father's hand, forgiveness in her eyes. Later, he would ask, how could this be? Roopa's eyes welled up with emotion. "I have forgiven my parents," she told her interviewer. And then Roopa spoke of the hardship and the difficulties of the oppression of the Dalit people. Her people. But she has found a new way. Now, her relationship with her mother and father is fully restored.

Today, she is employed as a clerk in a major department store in Bangalore. Not only does she earn a good wage, she has a new life she never thought possible. But her real dedication, she told George, is to help other women caught in a web of exploitation and abuse, to find their way out, into the light of a new day.

Our dramatic film, *Not Today*, is in the category of fiction. Our central character, Annika, is a fictional character. But if you look closely enough, there in the mind-numbing statistics on global slavery (the current number at twenty-seven million), you'll find real-world Annikas—rescued, restored, and empowered. Roopa Raju is one of them.

Her transformation inspired and motivated us to redouble our efforts.

CLIMBING FOR FREEDOM

When Cathey Anderson headed home with her husband, Mark, just after their Mount Whitney climb in 2011, it came to her like a blinding epiphany.

She knew about our work in India and the plight of the Dalits. An agriculture major in college, and a credentialed "ag" teacher in a country middle school, she spent time in Africa helping farmers increase their yields. She understood the great challenges of the developing world. Her heart broke for the women and children. The climb to the top of Whitney was a monumental physical challenge. She later said that without Mark's support and encouragement, she never would have made it.

Yet on their drive home from the highest peak of the continental United States, she turned to Mark and announced, "I want to climb Kili."

"Say again?" Mark asked, startled, not sure where in the world *this* came from.

Just that prior year, Mark had climbed Mount Kilimanjaro in Tanzania with several of his lifelong friends. He would later call it the most demanding thing he had ever done. At over 19,000 feet above sea level, Kilimanjaro pushed him further toward complete physical collapse than he had ever gone. The lack of oxygen made him retch with sickness—combine that with utter exhaustion and cold. He wondered, to this day, what was he thinking when he and his pals set out to conquer the frozen peak more than three and one-half miles above sea level. "Because it was there, I guess," he would say with a shrug. He turned to Cathey.

"Did you just say you want to climb Kili?" Mark turned his eyes off the road, looking to his wife for signs of sanity.

"Yes," she said, with steely resolve. Mark knew this look. He'd been married to her for a long time. Cathey continued.

"I don't usually speak like this, Mark. It's so weird. I can't shake it." Then almost timidly, she added, "It's as though God was speaking to me while we were on that mountain." Then she shared her reflections while she was climbing.

As they continued down the highway along California's Sierra Nevada mountain range, her purpose came into focus. "I want to recruit a bunch of women who think like I do, who care like I do . . . and we'll climb Kili together—all to encourage the people we know and trust who are making a difference all over the world. We'll work hard and raise a ton of money."

When Cathey climbed California's Mount Whitney to the summit, 14,500 feet above sea level, she tasted hardship. Physical pain. She felt the strong urge to quit. Now, she could not stop thinking about the stories of trafficking and human bondage. What she experienced on that mountain was like the pain of her life.

Sometime afterwards, her close friend Regina Bergeron gave her a book she had been reading: *Half the Sky*, written, as already mentioned, by the two Pulitzer Prize–winning journalists (and husband and wife), Nicholas Kristof and Sheryl WuDunn. (The title is an allusion to the proverb, "Women hold up half the sky.")

The authors' work for the *New York Times* captured international attention. The volume was something of a rebuke to the international media. They made

> As Cathey struggled to put one foot in front of the other on Mount Whitney, she contemplated the suffering of a world of forgotten people living in despair.

a strong case: in all the coverage that makes it into print—newspapers, magazines, books, and even the blogosphere—very little had been written about the global blight of trafficking: human slavery. They detailed the global epidemic.

Cathey devoured it.

The issues broke, then captured her heart. Women sold into slavery. Children forced into labor under horrible conditions. Agricultural workers held under oppressive debt, under the whips of cruel masters, suffering the separation of family, as slaves for generation after generation, just like pre–Civil War America. The world stood silent; the media more concerned with celebrity misbehavior and political grandstanding than the substantive issues of human rights. The demands of the Whitney climb pushed Cathey to her physical limits—and as she struggled to put one foot in front of the other both up and down the mountain, she contemplated the suffering of a world of forgotten people living in despair. People with no voice, especially the women and children.

That conversation was the birth of a new movement that is sweeping across America. They call it Freedom Climb.

On January 11, 2012, forty-eight women from all corners of the globe gathered at the base of Mount Kilimanjaro, including several who are working directly for organizations dedicated to rescuing and empowering the victims of human trafficking. It took six long days. But they set several records: they were the largest single female group ever to summit together. Ninety percent of the women made it to the top (unprecedented). And, they raised more than three hundred thousand dollars for the cause.

Their work has inspired other women to climb other mountains. This year, the core group will take on Mount Everest base camp in Nepal.

HELP THAT DOES NOT HURT

Make no mistake; the movement to free the Dalits in India has its critics.

In 2011, Rajiv Malhotra published his book *Breaking India*, in which he criticizes what he considers the invasion of India by well-meaning but misguided Westerners who misrepresent India's problems and exploit India's needs. He charges that agencies, particularly those funded by evangelical organizations, are taking advantage of India's social problems to advance their own cause. He also criticizes the Indian leaders who welcome Western influence and resources as accommodators—even "opportunists" and "Uncle Toms"—a reference to an old American pejorative, used to insult American slaves who cuddle up to their masters.

While the self-described researcher presents an interesting history of the historic clash between India and "Western" cultures like Germany, Great Britain, and the United States, he seems to overlook the monstrous violations of human rights not only in India but all over the world. We all recognize that we are dealing with a global problem. We have learned from *Half the Sky* and others that we are facing similar challenges right here in our own cities. Trafficking is an enormous problem in Los Angeles, Denver, Houston, San Francisco, and New York. We need to be aware of the potential for abuse in the world of charity, but withdrawing and throwing up our hands in despair won't help anyone.

Dr. Brian Fikkert and Steve Corbett have responded to this challenge in their pertinent bestseller, *When Helping Hurts* (Moody Publishers). The West earned its reputation through the years as a collection of colonial powers often disregarding the rights and needs as they occupied their "emerging" colonies. The American relief enterprise sometimes reflects that air of superiority and displays a lack of sensitivity to the real needs of their beneficiaries. They misunderstand the problem and worse, the cultural norms and local power structures. Donations sometimes never get to the people who need it the most. Robert Lupton calls it "Toxic Charity." It is not enough to simply transfer funds from a wealthy nation to a needy nation, and then feel satisfied that we've done our part.

> We are sensitive to the ways in which sadly, some of us have earned a reputation as "ugly Americans."

That's why our focus is a sustainable, long-term solution: education centers, safe houses, and economic development strategies developed and run by competent Indian leadership. We are sensitive to the ways in which sadly, some of us have earned a reputation as "ugly Americans." But it does not cause us to pull back or ignore either the gross violation of human dignity or the possibility of changing the system through focused, intentional action.

While some of the critics have a basis for identifying abuses in relief efforts gone wrong, the plight of the victims of trafficking is touching a nerve wherever the story told. The truth marches on. The cause gathers momentum.

Enter Passion 2013. New Year's Day 2013, 60,000 students (from seniors in high school through age twenty-five, from fifty-four countries and over two thousand college campuses) gathered in Atlanta for a conference called Passion 2013. Louis Giglio and his team made trafficking a primary cause for the conference to tackle as young students gathered to "Make Jesus Famous." They produced a powerful, emotionally charged thirty-minute documentary that captures essence of the problem. They raised money and awareness. President Barack Obama declared January 2013 "National Slavery and Human Trafficking Prevention Month." In his proclamation, he said, "We recognize the people, organizations and government entities that are working to combat human trafficking; and we recommit to bringing an end to this inexcusable human rights abuse."

Brent brought our film, *Not Today*, to the Catalyst Conference, a large gathering of church leaders from across the nation, and the showing met with great enthusiasm and high praise. Just a few weeks prior, Brent screened the film at the Urbana Student Missions Conference in St. Louis over the Christmas holidays. Sixteen thousand students attended the triennial conference sponsored by InterVarsity Christian Fellowship. Here are some of their comments reported by Christian Cinema:

"Gripping, informative movie that takes you into its world . . . makes you want to get involved to make a difference."

"Everyone should see this film. You cannot walk away unchanged."

"Heartbreaking and eye-opening . . . I am inspired to make a change."

"Wow! Should have warned us to bring Kleenex."

TODAY IN INDIA

But most important to us has been the response of India. Dr. D'souza considers the film to be the most powerful tool that has been created to date. It tells the story that is central to his vision for the nation.

> No one knew what would emerge from that electric gathering of Dalits in 2001. Now, more than ten years later, the movement has sparked a global awareness.

No one knew what would emerge from that electric gathering of Dalits in New Delhi back in 2001, so soon after the terrible attacks on September 11. At the time, Joseph's team debated whether or not he should accept the invitation. They covered his appearance with intense prayer. They knew, along with Dr. Udit Raj and Dr. K. P. Yohannan, on that day their lives were at risk.

Now, more than ten years later, the movement has sparked a global awareness. Schools are up and running. Today, many Dalit children receive a first-rate education and are learning English—the language of commerce. Legislatures entertain solutions proposed by smart, credentialed, articulate advocates. Women climb mountains. Mission agencies rally staff and supporters around the cause. Churches are popping up all over India. A bright, new, eager generation of Jesus-followers respond to His challenge to give a voice to the voiceless. Law schools are offering international and human rights courses, even majors. Musicians are writing songs. Writers write books. An American president declared a month dedicated to the cause.

A church made a movie.

That's not all.

More important: Slaves set free. The violated made whole. Souls redeemed. Children finding a future and a hope.

We are only beginning. There is so much to do. So many still in bondage.

Prime Minister, *Emancipate!*

NOTES

1. John 8:36.
2. Galatians 3:28.

Chapter 15

CENTENNIAL:
THE **NEXT 100 YEARS**

October 2012-California

I'M GOING TO CHALLENGE YOU with a question: Are you in? If not, what's holding you back? Take some time to think this one over.

If you visited our church today, you would find no trace of those tumultuous days when, with the framework for a new worship center barely out of the ground, our leadership seriously considered canceling the whole building project. They actually had hired a team of experts to determine the cost of tearing down the new structure, returning the space to an open lot. More hurdles came later: staff challenges; a global economic meltdown; a literal firestorm just miles from the church.

Those days are well behind us now.

On any given weekend, you'll find a beehive of broad-based ministries—but that's just the weekend. All week long, it never stops.

And now, as I write, it's official. Our church is one hundred years old.

THE DALITS OF ORANGE COUNTY

What you'll see around our campus is not busywork. It's all rooted in a vision for Global Freedom. The Dalit people are our inspiration here in Southern California. We have come to understand what these nearly 300 million men, women, and children are up against. For thousands of years, they have been told they have no value. They are subhuman. They are destined to be untouchable. Conversion to any other status or religion would be violation of the law, punished as a crime. They are caught in a system that denies them access to education, to worship, to economic advancement. They are banished from polite society. Ostracized. Condemned to menial labor. Without adequate compensation. In essence: captives. Indeed, many are slaves.

> For a growing number, this is *not* their "absolute destiny." Many have cast off the shackles of casteism.

From early childhood, they are told that this is all there is. Don't complain. Don't protest. Accept your lot. Keep yourself out of sight. Obscure. In the shadows. Extinguish any expectation you may have about a better life.

But now we know. For a growing number, this is *not* their "absolute destiny." Many have cast off the shackles of casteism and claim a new identity. They have embraced the possibilities of a new way of viewing the world. Against all odds, many have secured an education. They have been empowered to love and give. Literacy has opened their eyes and hearts to new, formerly unthinkable options. They have declared independence, tasted freedom. They have found spiritual healing and wholeness. And this is the essence of the Gospel of Jesus. Many now will tell you, with a light in their eyes and joy in their hearts, they have decided to follow this Jesus. I have met with them. Laughed with them. I have heard their stories. And now I understand . . .

Their story is ours. Here in California, we are a congregation of American Dalits who have found the same. Once *we* were lost, too. But now we are found. That's why we feel such a powerful connection.

FROM WILBERFORCE TO THE ORANGE GROVES

As we approached our one-hundred-year anniversary, I asked church member Craig Hodgkins to compile a book detailing our church's journey since those early days, back before World War I. It was in 1912 that a group of folks launched this ministry in what was then rural Yorba Linda.

For the next eight months, Craig and I worked together, reliving a full century of ministry in our town. Craig dived into the archives and interviewed countless people, producing a fine volume that got wide distribution.

The process connected me to our roots. And what hit me hard was the realization that our Global Freedom initiative is completely consistent with God's call on those folks who launched our ministry back when our town was known for its groves of oranges and grapefruit. The Marshburn family brought their generous spirit and love for God to those first gatherings. They would not only provide much of the resources needed to launch our church through their discipline of "tithing," they would also be the prime movers in launching what is today a major university and a global radio ministry that has for more than half a century broadcast the message of good news around the world. You will recognize some of the names of other charter families. The Nixons. The Truebloods. The Wests. Their Quaker tradition came to be called, simply, Friends.

They traced their roots back to William Wilberforce (heavily influenced by the Quaker movement in Great Britain), who championed the abolition of slavery by the British Parliament, beginning with the passage of the Slave Trade Act of 1807. That legislation became the basis for the comprehensive Slavery Abolition Act of 1833.

Wilberforce believed that his personal faith had moral implications. He stressed the importance of global awareness, and founded several mission agencies, including an outreach to India. He believed in the centrality and value of education.

Our founding families shared those values. They established a system of education for their children. They had a global vision. In those early days, they committed themselves to a high moral standard. They worshiped together, singing with full voice. They shared a vibrant, warm relationship with a loving God who redeems, heals, and empowers for a fulfilling life in community.

Through the years, they would impact our country and our world through the people who associated with the church. Others would be attracted to this ministry—some of them high profile.

GREAT IS HIS FAITHFULNESS

John Wimber, a singer and songwriter perhaps best known for his work with the popular 1960s duo The Righteous Brothers, came to our church with a chip on his shoulder. He knew he needed something. It was his wife, Carol, who believed they both needed God. So reluctantly, he showed up. It was the palpable reality of God's presence in the place that first broke through. When he finally dropped his guard, he turned his life over to Jesus and began to study the Bible. Before long, he was transformed into a dynamic Bible teacher. That was the beginning of a ministry career that would be best known for the launch of a movement that now circles the globe: The Vineyard.

An All-American in two sports at the University of Southern California, baseball and basketball, John Werhas missed a spot on the Los Angeles Lakers, but was drafted by the Los Angeles Dodgers and later traded to the California Angels. After he finished his professional career, he played some international baseball and then was recruited as a sportscaster with a Southern California NBC affiliate. Shortly after he married Kay, the newlyweds made an unexpected commitment to Jesus Christ. Soon, John was teaching Bible studies and emerged as a chaplain to professional athletes.

He would work closely with players and coaches, leading chapel services and Bible studies, counseling and praying with athletes and their families. Over time, he worked with all four Southern California professional football and baseball teams—the Dodgers, the Angels, the Lakers, the Rams, and later the Oakland Raiders.

And then he became pastor of our church.

John knew me as a professional trumpet player. He invited me to be part of his team, developing the worship program of a growing church, reaching out into a needy community with a message of hope. He mentored me. Coached me, as he did so many. We would shoot baskets together, plan together, laugh together, and pray together.

I am deeply grateful for John Werhas.

Our church became a place for strong men—business leaders; educators; professionals from medicine, law enforcement, finance, and law; firefighters; politicians; professional athletes; as well as musicians and performers. Our leadership loved to say it: "Real men follow Jesus." Our group became known as M.O.B.—Men of the Bible. We played all manner of sports , especially golf. Our men's outreach grew exponentially.

Stories of dramatic conversions proliferated.

One of my favorites was Bill Williams, a PhD in industrial psychology who had a successful career facilitating CEO forums for top-tier executives from some of the largest corporations in the nation. He trained facilitators to gather these high-profile men and women around a program of mutual support and encouragement, with explosive results. Then after a great run and impressive growth, a wealthy Wall Street tycoon acquired his company. He gladly retired. Shortly after that, Bill showed up at one of our men's weekend retreats. He'll tell you today, there was something missing in his life. He had all the success a man could ask for: a secure retirement, a great marriage, three prosperous sons (who brought him three fine daughters-in-law and a flock of grandkids), and high-level, meaningful friendships all over the world. But still, there was a void, a void that ached.

And in association with this collection of strong men who called themselves the M.O.B., he found what he was missing. One evening, on the invitation of a lively and energetic speaker at a weekend getaway, Bill stepped out of his seat and walked down to the front where he committed his life to Jesus.

He was sixty-one years old.

Today, he impacts other men, women, and children all over the world, including me.

As we celebrated one hundred years in 2012, we were amazed at how, on the surface at least, so much had changed. We utilize state-of-the-art technology, impacting much of what we do. Technology and methods have been perhaps the most obvious representation of change from the early days, other than the fact that we are all aging.

But our core values? They have remained the same since our founders first gathered together in a small church structure that cost just under $1,500 to build.

In a gathering of all the folks who have been touched by our ministry, we celebrated God's goodness and grace. We sang "Great Is Thy Faithfulness" with a genuine sense of conviction. But we also knew and understood that this milestone was not an ending point, but rather, a starting point.

We affirmed together that as good as the past has been, the best is yet to come.

PRANITHA'S STORY

Dr. Joseph D'souza has become an honorary associate pastor to our church. He brought some of his team to California to celebrate with us, and to get us current in our shared vision of changing a nation. Most memorable was Pranitha, a strikingly tall, attractive young woman with shining jet-black hair falling over her shoulders. Dressed in a brightly colored sari, she lit up the room with her smile. Joseph interviewed her in English, and she responded in our English language with a charm that captured the entire audience. Born a Dalit, she had no expectation that her life would be any better than her parents, who suffered the kind of indignities we have described many times in this book. But then, someone introduced her to one of our schools.

Today, Pranitha is a recent graduate of our DEC schools. Joseph asked about her future plans. She announced to us all the incredible news: she has been accepted to a fully accredited medical school in Hyderabad. In the next few years, she will be a practicing physician (like Joseph and Mariam's daughter, Beryl). As tears formed in her eyes and rolled down her cheeks, she thanked God for her new life.

Our people stood and applauded wildly, tears rolling down their cheeks, too.

A VISION FOR THE WORLD

When Richard Stearns finished his degree in neurobiology at Cornell University, he knew he loved science, but he loved business even more. That got him to the Wharton School, where he earned a prestigious MBA. The corporate opportunities came along, and he proved his mettle at the Gillette Company, then Parker Brothers, and on to Lenox (the manufacturer of fine china), where he became known for his ability to mobilize teams around business excellence. But when he was contacted to consider bringing his leadership skills to one of the largest nonprofit relief agencies in the world, it gave him pause. It sent him on a journey that sounds a whole lot like mine.

It was a professional move like none other in his stellar career to date. Rich's style included a focus on analytics, and when the offer to consider this position came through, he pulled the trigger and launched a thorough due diligence. He gathered all the data he could find. He spoke to his colleagues and friends. He interviewed the top tier leadership of the nonprofit. His due diligence also included serious prayer with his wife,

Reneé. Up until now, he hadn't really paid that much attention to the glaring disparity between haves and have-nots; between the full participants of the burgeoning global economy and the scarcities familiar to emerging nations. He had been a pretty serious Christian (or so he would say), but he had not really thought significantly about Jesus' claim that God's heart took the needy into special account. He had no real frame of reference: the notion that those who claim to be godly have a unique obligation to consider the needs of the poor, well, that had never been on his radar.

Just considering the position of president of a relief agency got him into a whole raft of literature. It also got him on an airplane. He had to see it for himself. His destination? Africa.

One day he sat with an orphaned child in a mud hut in Rakai, Uganda. He knew about the violence: the night invasions of terrorist groups, gun-toting children perpetrating unthinkable brutality, killings, rapes, and burnings. But now, he sat face-to-face with a young boy whose parents had been taken in the crossfire. It became personal. He felt God's presence there, just as I did in the Corporate Stay Hotel. That sense of presence became a calling.

Rich Stearns's understanding of the Gospel up until that moment was missing something, he wrote. Something critical, essential, foundational. He had always thought the Gospel of Jesus Christ to be a proposition either to accept or reject. We receive the "good news," embrace it, and we become members of a new community, with an eternal destiny secured. But Stearns realized that while this concept has real merit, it also overlooks something profound. Rich thought, "Would it be enough for me to share a message with this little Ugandan orphan boy and get him to simply shake his head yes, affirming that he believed my message?" Important? Yes. Adequate? No.

What about this child's future? Who will care for him? What about safety? Nutrition? Medicine? And then, what about education? What about literacy? What about his sense of identity? His belief in the possibilities of a world, now so dangerous, but also filled with potential? What about the cycle of violence? What about the systemic injustice that lines the pockets of thugs who rule by force, but leave the rest without?

What about the infestations that make infant mortality rates soar? Or the AIDS that takes too many mothers and fathers from their children? What about water

> Rich Stearns realized that his "Gospel" fell painfully short.

that is not only scarce, it also crammed with impurities? What happens when the storms come, the fires rage, and crops fail? What then?

All of these questions and more filled the mind and heart of the executive whose company made and sold fine china, crystal glassware, and delicate figurines for upscale homes on the right side of town, filling them with "treasures." Rich Stearns realized that his "Gospel" fell painfully short. He calls it a "hole in the Gospel," which became the title of his award-winning book.[1]

His book makes a profound point. And as Rich Stearns thought it through, he realized that he had simply accepted a version of the Gospel that is more a reflection of affluent North American culture than a reflection of the heart of God. Jesus' question, "where were you when I was hungry, naked and in prison" haunted him, as it has haunted me. And when you are sitting across the table from the child of hunger in the heart of Africa or in a Pipe Village slum; in the aftermath of terrible violence, where whatever water might be handy is also contaminated and where the schools are nowhere to be found—it all closes in. You are stumped. At the end of yourself. Aware that all your glittering and abundant resources are not enough.

You pause. And then God meets you there.

And that's how it works.

God met Rich Stearns.

He met me, too.

If this has never happened to you, go there and see.

He'll meet you, too.

To the surprise and shock of his colleagues and fellow CEOs, Stearns took the job at World Vision in 1999. Since then, he has presided over unprecedented growth. World Vision raised nearly three billion dollars in 2011 for global relief.

"WE'LL SEE WHAT LOVE CAN DO"

Aaron Blanton never stops creating. He's been to India. Sunday after Sunday, he leads our worship. He was made for it. He draws us in. And now he, along with this friend, James Tealy, has written a new original track that you will hear as the credits roll at the end of our film, *Not Today*. It is inspired. He has captured the essence of what we've been trying to say in these pages.

I could sit here and pretend I didn't know
I could move on and you'd just assume I had to go
But now that I have met you
I gotta take the chance
I could turn and walk away

And frankly, that's what most of us do—"turn and walk away." It was the Good Samaritan who stopped to care for the victim of a roadside beating and theft. The others, according to Jesus, walked on by. Aaron has met the children in the slums and in the schoolyard. Aaron goes on . . .

But I've seen what love can do
When you set it free
Pick up the pieces and make it new
Break through the walls between us
And I know if we let go of this
Fear that held us here and make a move
We'll see what love can do
I could hide away inside this American dream
And tell myself it's someone else's destiny

But now that I have held you
I've gotta take the chance
I could turn and walk away
I'm tired of saying no to the truth
That I can be the change and the proof
That love is alive and grace is still amazing

Amazing grace positions Aaron to take a chance.

You have been with me now on quite a journey. I've shared my story the best I know how. I took you with me into that dark place in my life when I lost my job; everything I considered secure was gone. Our church nearly imploded just as construction had built momentum on our campus. And then we walked through a time of reconciliation and rebuilding. We made the commitment to be outward focused, not inward or self-absorbed. We knew we needed to trust God on levels we had never known before.

And then you came via the printed page to India with me. You now know the Dalits, what they have suffered; you know something of their longing for freedom. You have met some of the heroes, some who have given their lives to the cause. You know there are schools being built, and children who understand a Gospel with no hole in it. You have been with us as a movie was made, from the writing of the script to the scouting of location sites to the casting, filming, and postproduction. You understand that this is way more than a movie for the purpose of entertainment.

You understand our cause. You know that there is a whole world in need. Men, women, and children are being abused and violated, bought and sold. The American Civil War may have officially ended slavery in America, but it did not solve the problems of casteism or racism or global slavery or human trafficking. Parents struggle to feed their families, and they hope for the possibilities of education. Spiritual poverty is more than matched by physical, intellectual, economic, and psychological poverty. But now that we are here, together, I want to be very direct.

ARE YOU READY?

I remember well when I came to understand that Jesus' words to the formerly lame beggar were really for me. "Get up, Matthew. Take up your mat. Walk!" God got my attention. As He told Joshua, He told me: "Be strong. Take courage. Do not be afraid." As Moses stood before the great Pharaoh, he cried, "Let my people go!" God has prompted Joseph D'souza and me to declare the same.

> Taking note of the things that Jesus noticed, aligning myself with His work in my neighborhood and around the world is the reason I was created.

I have met people who are longing for leaders who will stand up to power and make the same cry. "Freedom!" Lose the chains. Break the shackles. Set my people free. We have been empowered with a Gospel that has that transformational impact, in this life and the next.

I have been given a calling for which I am willing to spend my life, even if it means my life. And when I touched down at Begumpet Airport on that watershed day, it happened. In laying down that old life, that old way of thinking, I found the very thing that has made me alive—to a whole new world.

I have no interest in promoting or perpetuating "religion." I was a "poster boy" for American Christianity. But that will never be enough. In fact, I believe now that it was like climbing an endless ladder that was leaning against the wrong wall.

Now, I understand that finding the heartbeat of God, taking note of the things that Jesus noticed, aligning myself with His work in my neighborhood and around the world is the reason I was created in the first place.

And now, as we close out our book, I don't want you to miss it.

I feel compelled to ask you the same questions that have haunted me:

Where have you been? What has been demanding your time? Your gifts? Your talent? Your interests? Your passion? Your money? Your art? Your creative energy? Your relational skill? Your worship? Your voice? Your heart?

Your treasure?

Fine china? Crystal glassware? Elegant figurines? Rich Stearns got it. Ask him if he would ever go back.

Joseph D'souza made an audacious claim. I believe it came from God. "We are part of a movement that will eliminate the evils of the caste system in India."

Can you see it?

Does it break your heart? Does it stir something deep inside?

If so, join us.

Let's change the world.

God simply wants to hear you say, along with me, "I'm in."

I am so in.

NOTE

1. Richard Stearns, *A Hole in our Gospel: What Does God Expect of Us?* (Nashville: Thomas Nelson, 2009). The Evangelical Christian Publishers Association named it the Christian Book of the Year in 2010.

Epilogue

By Kenneth Kemp

WHEN MATTHEW CORK invited me to coauthor a book with him about Global Freedom, I did not hesitate for a moment.

In our first meeting, I was aware. I knew about the audacious vision to eliminate the caste system in India. I had been introduced to Dr. Joseph D'souza. The Dalit Freedom Movement fascinated me. I watched the church move from near disaster to high-energy focus. The generous, selfless commitment of the people of Friends Church of Yorba Linda, California, staggers the imagination.

The prospect of devoting a year to studying the particulars, gathering the information, verifying facts and figures, and then working with Matthew to tell the story energized me in profound ways. Before long, I packed my bags for Hyderabad, India. I traveled all over the country with the producer, director, and cinematographer as we planned to film a movie about the plight of the Dalits, *Not Today*. I walked the slums and the schools and the bustling streets of India's cities and villages. For most of the fifteen-hour train ride to Kolkata, I wrote from my "bunk." I spoke with teachers and students, government officials and mission executives. The people of India disarmed and charmed me. The children captured my heart. I compiled a reading list. Within weeks, we went to work.

Most everyone who spends enough time with Global Freedom to grasp its scope finds himself or herself transformed. I am no exception. Matthew and I spent innumerable hours in lively conversation reliving the journey. I interviewed countless others. We read books. We traveled. We googled. We journaled.

Matthew tells his story in first person. It is nothing short of an amazing journey. In our collaboration, Matthew gave me great latitude as a writer. He encouraged me with the freedom to express the journey in my own literary terms. We added lots of historical background. We aimed for depth and breadth. But make no mistake: this is Matthew's story. These reflections come from his heart and mind.

But even more, *Why Not Today* is a God story. A powerful God story.

I was simply given the distinct honor of going along for the ride.

And what a ride.

WHAT CAN I DO NOW?

WHY A BOOK AND A MOVIE ABOUT HUMAN TRAFFICKING?

The simple answer is: "None of us is free if one of us is enslaved."
Now you know. It's time to take action. Time to commit.

WHAT CAN ONE OF US DO TO MAKE A DIFFERENCE?

From supporting the education of a Dalit child to helping build schools in India to working alongside groups focused on ending slavery everywhere, you or your organization can take a first step toward making a difference today!

Here are some tangible, powerful ways you can become part of a growing movement to make a lasting, sustainable impact on one of the world's most destructive evils.

Explore. Read. Learn. Sign up. Show up.

FREE A CHILD

For more than a decade, the Dalit Freedom Network (DFN) has been helping educate Dalit children in India as part of their work as the leading voice of justice for the Dalits.

Through education, the opportunity for freedom is born. Each child who attends school discovers they were created with a purpose. And through education, they can lift themselves and their families from endless generations of discrimination and abuse.

Help free and empower one child or many children. You can provide an educational opportunity for a Dalit child in India for just $30 a month. Make a difference: free a child today! (www.nottodayresources.com)

FUND A SCHOOL

According to a 2006 United Nations Special Report on the Right to Education, "Dalit children face considerable hardships in schools, including discrimination, discouragement, exclusion, alienation, physical and psychological abuse, and even segregation, from both their teachers and fellow students."

By building 1,000 schools specifically for Dalit children, the Dalit Freedom Network provides a setting without these negative factors. Friends Church, which produced Not Today, is in the process of building 200 schools over a ten-year period.

Through the Not Today Coalition, you can help change the future for an entire community of Dalit children. At the cost of $100,000 per school, your church, advocacy group, or business might fund a school. Perhaps your school, youth group, or organization wants to join with others to build a school. Maybe your family wants to contribute. However much or little you give will go a long way in changing the future in India. (www. nottodayresources.com)

FIGHT SLAVERY

In the minds of many Americans, slavery ended with the conclusion of the Civil War. If only that were true. If you've seen Not Today, you've experienced the reality of this evil in our world today.

It is time for every person to stand up and say, Not today. Slavery must end and it must end now. Share Not Today with your friends in the cities where the movie is playing, or on DVD, and let them know the importance of seeing this movie.

Then step up and join the fight. If not us, who? And if not now, when? It's time to end trafficking . . . today.

WORK WITH OUR GLOBAL PARTNERS

We are grateful for the support of these organizations that are actively involved in helping bring justice and mercy to a hurting world. Visit any or all of these organizations to discover how you can help make a difference in the world!

The A21 Campaign

The A21 Campaign comprises individuals, organizations, government officials, and everyday people who are committed to one goal: to abolish slavery in the twenty-first century. A21 works through prevention, protection, prosecution, and partnership in countries around the world. VISIT thea21campaign.org.

Abolition International

Abolition International is committed to integrity and excellence as they create a collaborative community of inspired abolitionists who are determined to end sex slavery in our lifetime. They advocate for survivors of sex slavery by promoting quality standards, affecting policy, ensuring sustainable aftercare models, and engaging communities in life-changing educational opportunities both domestically and abroad. VISIT abolitioninternational.org.

Aglow International

Aglow International is a transformational kingdom culture committed to seeing God's will done on earth as it is in heaven by raising up champions and warriors across the earth who will bring freedom to the oppressed. These champions provide opportunities for everyone in their spheres of influence to grow into radiant relationships with each other as well as with the Father, the Son, and the Holy Spirit. VISIT aglowinternational.org.

Dalit Freedom Network

Believing injustices against the Dalit people in India must end, DFN is a human-rights organization striving to stop human trafficking and child labor, and make slavery history in India. This NGO represents a vast network of justice-minded, modern-day abolitionists committed to bringing freedom to history's longest-standing oppressed people group. VISIT dalitnetwork.org.

Focus on the Family
Focus on the Family is a global Christian ministry dedicated to helping families thrive. They believe that human life is created by God in His image. Christians are therefore called to defend, protect, and value all human life, including those who are enslaved or trapped in systemic oppression. VISIT focusonthefamily.com.

Freedom Climb
Today, millions of women and children around the world are enslaved, trafficked, and oppressed. The Freedom Climb is an opportunity for women in all stages, ages, and places to be a voice for these women and children. The climb is a symbolic gesture of the struggle to freedom they face every day. Forty-four women from all over the world recently met in Nepal and trekked to the base camp of Mt. Everest and then summited the neighboring peak of Kala Phattar. When the climbers stand at the top of Kala Phattar, they are declaring life and freedom for those who cannot speak for themselves. VISIT thefreedomclimb.net.

IMB | South Asian Peoples
The International Mission Board is an entity of the Southern Baptist Convention, dedicated to making disciples of each and every nation in fulfillment of the Great Commission. IMB South Asian Peoples long to see a vast multitude from every South Asian nation, tribe, people, and language redeemed and worshiping the Risen Christ. They labor constantly to better the lives of South Asians today, tomorrow, and for all eternity. VISIT southasianpeoples.imb.org/NotToday.

Live58

Live58 is an unprecedented alliance of Christians working together to end extreme poverty in our lifetime by living out the True Fast of Isaiah 58. VISIT live58.org.

International Justice Mission

This human-rights agency rescues victims of slavery, sexual exploitation, and other forms of violent oppression. IJM lawyers, investigators, and aftercare professionals work with local officials to secure immediate victim rescue and aftercare, to prosecute perpetrators and to ensure that public justice systems—police, courts, and laws—effectively protect the poor. VISIT ijm.org.

National Hispanic Christian Leadership Conference

The National Hispanic Christian Leadership Conference is the nation's largest Christian Hispanic organization, unifying, serving, and representing millions in the Hispanic born-again community via more than 40,000 member churches. NHCLC reconciles the vertical and horizontal of the Christian message through these Seven Directives: Life, Family, Great Commission, Stewardship, Justice, Education, and Youth. VISIT nhclc.org.

Operation Mobilization USA

A Christian mission organization, Operation Mobilization inspires and equips believers to expand God's kingdom. OM works around the world with 6,100 missionaries from more than 100 nations working in more than 110 countries and onboard an ocean-going missions ship. OM USA is the entry point from the U.S. into that mission movement. VISIT omusa.org.

OM Ministries India

The India Group of OM Ministries works to transform lives and communities in India by equipping people to share the love of God in word and in deed. Founded in 1964, OM India focuses on spiritually enriching lives, training and equipping pastors, training young people to live effective lives, empowering the underprivileged and oppressed, standing for social liberty and human rights, and uplifting women. VISIT omindia.org.

SAVN.tv

SAVN.tv is a new Internet call-to-action website with programming that reflects the services that the Salvation Army provides worldwide. Most people know the Salvation Army as a "red kettle." What they don't know is the multitude of programs, campaigns, relief, and life-changing opportunities offered by the Salvation Army. The Salvation Army has been serving suffering humanity globally since 1865. The Salvation Army meets the needs of the poor and vulnerable at the point of need without discrimination. VISIT savn.tv/human-trafficking.

Youth With A Mission (YWAM)

An international volunteer movement of Christians from many backgrounds, cultures, and traditions, YWAM is dedicated to knowing God and making Him known. Started in 1960, YWAM operates in more than 1,000 locations in 180 countries, with a staff of more than 18,000 people. VISIT ywam.org.

ADDITIONAL WEB RESOURCES

HumanTrafficking.org—News, updates, and resources from around the world

InvisibleChildren.com—Advocates on behalf of children impacted by strife in East and Central Africa

Justice-Generation.com—Hotline to report human trafficking; connects with other advocacy organizations

NotforSaleCampaign.org—Fights modern-day worker enslavement globally through education, advocacy and business development

MORE READING

ALERT — *may contain graphic, disturbing content.*

Siddharth Kara, *Bonded Labor: Tackling the System of Slavery in South Asia* (New York: Columbia University Press, 2012).

Joseph D'souza, *Dalit Freedom Now and Forever: The Epic Struggle for Dalit Emancipation* (Washington, DC: Dalit Freedom Network, 2005).

Daniel Walker, *God in a Brothel: An Undercover Journey into Sex Trafficking and Rescue* (Downers Grove, IL: InterVarsity Press, 2011).

Nicholas D. Kristof and Sheryl WuDunn, *Half the Sky: Turning Oppression into Opportunity for Women Worldwide* (New York: Vintage, 2010).

Kevin Bales, Zoe Trodd, and Alex Kent Williamson, *Modern Slavery: The Secret World of 27 Million People* (Oxford: Oneworld Publications, 2009).

David Batstone, *Not for Sale: The Return of the Global Slave Trade—and How We Can Fight It* (New York: HarperOne, 2010).

Dillon Burroughs and Charles Powell, *Not in My Town: Exposing and Ending Human Trafficking and Modern-Day Slavery* (Birmingham, AL: New Hope Publishers, 2011).

Sharon Hendry, *Radhika's Story: Surviving Human Trafficking* (London: New Holland Publishers, 2010).

Victor Malarek, *The Natashas: The Horrific Inside Story of Slavery, Rape, and Murder in the Global Sex Trade* (New York: Skyhorse Publishing, 2011).

Mary Frances Bowley, *The White Umbrella: Walking with Survivors of Sex Trafficking* (Chicago: Moody Publishers, 2012).

Brian Fikkert and Steve Corbett, *When Helping Hurts: How to Alleviate Poverty Without Hurting the Poor…and Yourself* (Chicago: Moody Publishers, 2012).

Eric Metaxas, *Amazing Grace: William Wilberforce and the Heroic Campaign to End Slavery* (San Francisco: HarperOne, 2007).

Carolyn Custis James, *Half the Church: Recapturing God's Global Vision for Women* (Grand Rapids: Zondervan, 2010).

Os Guinness, *The Call: Finding and Fulfilling the Central Purpose of Your Life* (Nashville: Thomas Nelson, 2003).

Timothy Keller, *Generous Justice: How God's Grace Makes Us Just* (New York: Dutton, 2012).

N.T. Wright, *Evil and the Justice of God* (Downers Grove, IL: IVP Books, 2009).

Randy Alcorn, *If God Is Good: Faith in the Midst of Suffering and Evil* (Colorado Springs: Multnomah, 2009).

Philip Yancey, *Where Is God When It Hurts?* (Grand Rapids: Zondervan, 1990).

Zach Hunter, *Be the Change: Your Guide to Freeing Slaves and Changing the World* (Grand Rapids: Zondervan, 2011).

Jim Wallis and Sojourners, *Justice for the Poor* (Grand Rapids: Zondervan, 2010).

FILMS: DOCUMENTARIES AND DRAMAS
Documentaries

The Day My God Died (PBS, 2008)—PBS-produced look at sex slavery.

The Human Experience (Grass Roots Films, 2008)—A band of brothers travels the world asking the "big questions" about life and its meaning.

Science of Evil (National Geographic, 2008)—Explores evil from diverse perspectives and places.

Not My Life (Worldwide, 2012)—*Lifetime* film about human trafficking.

Call + Response (Fair Trade, 2008)—Features interviews with former US secretary of state Madeleine Albright, actress-activist Ashley Judd, many more.

Dramas

Amazing Grace: The Movie (Bristol Bay, 2007)—The story of William Wilberforce's long fight to end the African slave trade to England.

Gandhi (Columbia Pictures, 1982; recent widescreen and Blu-Ray editions available)—The Oscar-winning biopic stars Ben Kingsley, Martin Sheen, and a very young Daniel Day-Lewis in a small role.

Trade of Innocents (Dean River, 2012)—Mira Sorvino and Dermot Mulroney star in this drama about human trafficking.

Acknowledgments

THERE ARE MANY I wish to thank. Jay Hoff convinced me to go to India. It changed my life forever. The elders who served since that day have believed from the beginning that this unlikely vision was of God. Brent Martz, Brian Ignatowski, Stuart Nichols, Mike Gadd, and Rick Underwood were there when I said, "We will build 200 schools." They have never wavered. Thank you for calling me crazy and then joining me on this amazing journey. Ken Kemp, for saying yes to India and helping to tell a story that needed to be told. You believed, and then you stayed with it—all the way. Janet Allen, for helping me to manage my life. But above all the rest, thank you to my life partner, Mardi, and our three phenomenal kids: Nolan, Sophie, and Ella.

—**Matthew Cork**

THANK YOU, Joseph D'souza, for first articulating the vision with such precision and passion; for your courageous stand; for your steadfast commitment to Dalit Freedom and to us. You and your tenacious team are changing a nation. Lives are and will continue to be transformed. You inspired our story. Udit Raj reviewed the narrative of the Delhi march of 2001, and generously offered his suggestions so that we got it right. Leah Kadwell was indispensable as a friend, resource, encourager, and meticulous reader. Jay Hoff, Alan Amaviska, Mike Gadd, and John Cone were there with information, zeal, and encouragement. Brent Martz never let go—your imprint on the movie makes it the fine messenger it is; your diligence and tireless focus spilled over to our book. David Mechem never stopped believing, or networking. Bill Williams asked all the right questions, smiling all the way. Lorry Kemp, thank you for reading with enthusiasm, never faltering from the first day in your conviction that this book will find a wide audience. Robert Wolgemuth understood what writers need to hear. Andrew Wolgemuth fell in love with India, and then our book. Duane Sherman took the risk because he believed in the cause and then he made it his own. Barnabas Piper brought energy and focus, building a bridge with the *Not Today* promotion team, and then carried his enthusiasm into the marketplace. Betsey Newenhuyse, a true professional, polished the prose and made it shine. Mike and Cindy Stein, Mark and Cathey Anderson, Randy and Lori Degler, Harry and Elaine Ellis, Andrew Scott, and Regina Bergeron all kept the fire stoked.

Thank you Matthew (Cork), for tapping into my gifts, my hopes, and my dreams; for taking me to India and introducing me to this movement that has transformed so many lives, including mine. And most of all, thank you Carolyn, for reading and rereading and listening long, for laughing and crying with me, for praying, and for understanding both my victories and defeats; for standing next to me all these years and believing that the best is what God has in mind.

—**Kenneth Kemp**

DALIT FREEDOM NETWORK

Dalit Freedom Network (DFN) is a justice-minded organization that champions freedom for 250 million Dalit people in India. The Dalits, often identified by the demeaning labels of "untouchables" and "outcastes," are history's longest standing oppressed people group.

The Dalits also comprise the largest number of victims of India's number one social problem—human trafficking. Since 2002 DFN and its India partners have been answering the pleas of Dalit leaders to "BE OUR VOICE!" "FREE OUR CHILDREN!" and "FREE OUR WOMEN!" through a "transformed community" model that provides education, economic development, healthcare, and social justice advocacy and intervention, with a goal to end Dalit apartheid and make slavery history in India.

Theirs is a story that needs to be told.

Dalitnetwork.org

CHECK OUT THESE TITLES

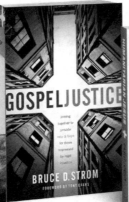

When Helping Hurts
How to Alleviate Poverty Without
Hurting the Poor . . . and Yourself

Gospel Justice
Joining Together to Provide
Help and Hope for those
Oppressed by Legal Injustice

Humanitarian Jesus
Social Justice and the Cross

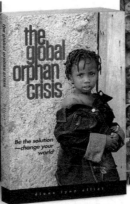

The White Umbrella
Walking with
Survivors of Sex Trafficking

The Global Orphan Crisis
Be the Solution,
Change Your World

Just a Minute
In the Heart of a Child, One
Moment ... Can Last Forever

Also available as ebooks

MOODY
PUBLISHERS

www.MoodyPublishers.com